The Hills of Adonis

A Quest in Lebanon

The Hills of
ADONIS

A Quest in Lebanon

COLIN THUBRON

with photographs by the author

LITTLE, BROWN AND COMPANY   BOSTON   TORONTO

With remembrance of
Carol

Contents

Northern Lebanon

al-Mina
TRIPOLIS
Qubbet el Bedawi

Nahr Abu Ali

Zghorta

Ehden

Kannoubin
Dimah   Hadchit   Bechere
Batroun   Kadisha

L I B A

Amschit
Belaat
Jbail
(Byblos)   Fidar
Muhnaqa
Nahr Ibrahim (Adonis)
Akura

Aphaca

Mediterranean Sea

Ghineh

Meyrouba   Faraya
Jounie
Nahr el Leban
Qalat Fakra
Sarba   Reyfoun
Jeita
Nahr el Kelb (Dog)   Baskinta

BEIRUT

Broumana

Baabda
Kfar Selouan

Bhamdoun
Sofar
Qabb Elias

Yammouneh
Lake

Chlifa

M O N T

Jebel Kesrouan

Jebel Sannin

Niha
Fourzol
Kerak
ZAHLE
Chtaura
To Damascus
Deir el Ghazel

BAALBE
(HELIOPOLIS

S Y R I A

Mediterranean Sea

Nahr Damour

Deir el Kamar
Beit-ed-din
Baaklin•
•Simkaniye
•Mouchtara
Amatour•
Maaser-
es-Chouf

•Barouk

Nahr Litani

Mejdel Anjar•
Anjar
(Chalcl.

To
Damascus

Nahr Barouk

Joun •
•Deir Moukalles
Deir
Machmouche
•Borri

Nahr Awali

SAIDA
(SIDON)
Qalat Abu
l'Hassan

•Jezzine

Jebel Niha Jebel Barouk

Nahr Litani

•Rachaya

Sayadet el Mantara

•Yohmor

Sarafand•

H E R M O N

•Adlun

•Nabatyet

Marjayoun•

Nahr Litani

Beaufort
Castle

N

•Joweiya

•Ain Baal

Nahr Naqab

Kana•

Tibnin•

0		5		10 miles

0	5	10 kilometres

Jebel Amel

•Bint Jbail

Southern
Lebanon

SRAEL

Illustrations

From Photographs by the Author

Acknowledgements

THE AUTHOR is grateful to the publishers of the following works for permission to reprint excerpts: *The Poems of Sappho*; Trs. P. Maurice Hill (Staples Press). *The Greek Bucolic Poets*; Trs. A. S. F. Gow (C.U.P.). *The Iliad*; Homer; Trs. E. V. Rieu (Penguin Books). *Theocritus, Bion and Moschus*; Trs. Arthur S. Way (C.U.P.). *The Syrian Goddess*; Lucian; Trs. Prof. Herbert A. Strong (Constable & Co.), and to Miss Kathleen Raine for the lines from 'The Goddess' from *Living in Time* (Poetry London, Nicholson & Watson, 1946).

1. The Quest

Some worship her as queen of angels, Venus of the sea,
House of gold, palace of ivory,
Gate of heaven and rose of mystery,
Inviolate and ever-virgin earth,
Daughter of time and mother of eternity.

Kathleen Raine: *The Goddess*

O F ALL THE GODS conceived by ancient men, the last to pass away were those divinities of sun and earth who dominated the Semitic world. Because they represented most nearly the needs and instincts of mankind, they remained behind long after their images had been broken: rebellious, archetypal giants.

Such a deity was the love goddess, born between the Two Rivers, who came to Lebanon and wedded with a corn-spirit. The Semites called her Astarte, and worshipped her, with her lover Adonis, as the prime movers of life, whose veins and sinews were the fields and vines of men. But to the Greeks Adonis was a mortal, killed by a wild boar in a valley of Lebanon. Astarte, they said, had bargained for his soul against the powers of the underworld, and such was the force of love that he was sent back to her on earth for that part of the year when the streams are full and the fields green.

The Semites portrayed Astarte plainly, as an earth goddess, or as an hieratic queen seated among lions. But the Greeks, who knew of her fertility rites in Cyprus, called her Aphrodite and brought her cult to Athens for their childless king. With the passing of centuries they sheared her of her early powers and endowed her with the sapling grace of the Venus de Milo, with human qualities and a fickle heart. So she lost track of her origins, the divine energy failed, and to all appearances she vanished with the classical era.

But the gods mock such history, disguise themselves and seek new refuges; and if Aphrodite, who was herself the source of life, never really died, she would remain most surely in the mountains of Lebanon, where she first loved and was best worshipped. The hillsmen are a mosaic of races, but all truculent and passionate, and love and rebirth and the growth of trees and children are a primal blessing.

If this is true, a journey through Lebanon attains a special character. Not only is it a beautiful and diversified land, but it is the country of resurrection, where Adonis rises every year from the sad halls of Persephone. Death is familiar, resurrection a mystery; so Lebanon becomes worthy of deep exploration, in particular among the artefacts of her past and in the memory of her people. To drive through such a land would be to receive no sense of it, for Lebanon is half the size of Wales and is best seen as centuries of people knew it, on foot or on a donkey. For this reason I trusted in the hospitality of the *ahl al-Jebal*, 'the people of the mountain', by walking alone through the country; and besides, a goddess must be approached carefully, and with humility.

The worship of Aphrodite and Adonis was strongest in the region of the Giblites in north Lebanon, but their cult pervaded the whole land and might be found in obscure places. So I decided to start my search in the fishing-towns of the south, in Tyre and Sidon and Sarepta—incantatory names; pass eastward into the core of the mountains and the high, shallow valley which the Romans called Hollow Syria; from there to Baalbec and the cedar groves, descending at last to the holy country of Byblos.

The search for so many-faceted a divinity will entail being led astray, demanding, as it does, a long walk down the corridors of time and thought. The conclusions will be personal and the quest, of course, will not be satisfied, because its goal is sacred; but the purpose will remain to explore the country where love first saw beauty, and to gather up whatever stray garlands have been left behind.

2. The Earth Mother

Her lament is for a great river, where no willows grow,
Her lament is for a field, where corn and herbs grow not,
Her lament is for a pool, where fishes grow not,
Her lament is for a thicket, where no reeds grow.
Babylonian hymn, *Lament of the Flutes for Tammuz*

IT IS ALMOST SPRING, and the god has returned to earth.

Out of the south to the Taurus mountains comes a Mediterranean wind. The descent to the sea, by all ways, is beautiful and solitary, and the river valleys twine slowly down the hills as if prolonging the prospect of the green Cilician plain. From here the coast curves eastward to Iskenderun and Syria, and meets the Lebanese mountains where they rise from the desert. From Tripolis to Beirut the shore is suffocated by thriving towns of unrepentant plainness, but a few miles further south it is given back to rocks and orchards; lemon groves spread inland and Sidon stands on the sea.

The contrast with Beirut is complete, for Sidon is secretive and seems to have grown from the waves. At a distance it might, but for its minarets, be any Calabrian fishing-town, with mellow walls and tiled roofs.

The older city is on the tip of the headland; the sun only reaches it by accident, so narrow are its streets, and the sandstone blocks which the Turks carved shed a soft agelessness. In dark stores sit craftsmen with deft fingers. Their world is still provincial and oriental. Arabic music sounds from the cafés, and men sit out in the evening in slippers and nightcaps by the balm of the sea.

In the seventeenth century the emir Fakr ed Din, who ruled the Lebanon alone, built caravanserais and a palace in the city, and encouraged trade with France. Momentarily Sidon prospered and became the port of Damascus, but with the departure of the European trade mission, and an earthquake in 1837, it declined again, and the emir's stones were dismantled and set up for humbler uses. Only his largest khan, the Fransawi, is well preserved, now an orphanage for girls of the Sisters of St

Joseph: a courtyard with a burst of lemon trees in its centre and a wide pool. Around it runs a double-tiered portico of Arabic arches, heavy and masculine, where flowers creep, and where the stone rain-vents are all in place; and in the storage-rooms and stables, whose silence is deepened by the whispers of children, the tethering hoops for camels are still in their sockets.

Offshore a Crusader castle stands, linked to the headland by an arched causeway which has twice been swept away in recent years. On one side hewn stones stare greenly from the vault of the sea; on the other a silted reef scatters the waves. The castle has a frail, clean look, and even after one has smoothed one's hands over the thickness of its walls and looked down from the eastern tower, it is hard to envisage it as a building of military strength. On stormy days the sea breaks over its southern ramparts, which have been levelled to a paved quay. Headless lions dance on the consoles of the entrance-gate. Rusted cannon nestle in the sand. And in the walls lie grey and pink granite columns, set by the Crusaders against sapping, but brought from Egypt long ago, perhaps for a temple to Melqart or for that 'temple of great size owned by the Sidonians' of which Lucian wrote, dedicated to Astarte, but now vanished.

Sidon seems wholly mediaeval. Yet the Book of Genesis calls her 'the first-born of Canaan', the oldest city of those tribes who crossed the desert in the fourth millennium, and whom the Greeks named 'Phoenicians'. It was perhaps they who first brought the Great Goddess from the east, and it was they who made Lebanon her home and diffused her cult through the Mediterranean.

Sidon is built as the Phoenicians loved to build, on a spit of land with an island close by. Here they raised a small port and surrounded it with orchards which are still famous, and on the lower slopes of the hills grew up an inland city. It was not the earliest of the Phoenician towns, but was one of the first to establish a dominion along the coast in a time when history and myth are blended. Belus, the doyen of Phoenician kings, is only another name for Baal; and Agenor, legendary founder of Tyre and Sidon, is himself a half-god.

The cities which grew to maturity along the shore did not cling together as would be expected of tiny states among powerful neighbours, but were jealous and exclusive. They were Semitic to the heart. Eager and opportunist, enterprising traders and slave-dealers, their people did not look far beyond tomorrow, but grasped life as it came. Their artistic inspiration

'The Mourning Aphrodite': Seleucid statuette in limestone, 3¾ ins. high. (*Bibliothèque Nationale, Paris.*)

The idyllic view of Adonis: Graeco-Roman bronze. In one hand he holds a grain of incense, in the other a censer. (*Bibliothèque Nationale, Paris.*)

Sidon: The Castle of the Sea

Tyre: Byzantine sarcophagi

they drew and refined from Egypt and Mesopotamia. But their craftsmanship was superb. Homer calls them 'skilled in all things'. His heroes fought in Phoenician armour and their wives were dressed in Sidonian robes. The gold-rimmed bowl which Menelaus gave to Telemachus had been the property of a Phoenician king, and the prize which Achilles presented in the funeral games of Patroclus was 'a mixing-bowl of silver, chased . . . the loveliest thing in the world, for Sidonian craftsmen wrought it cunningly, and Phoenician traders sailed it over the misty sea, and landed it in port, and gave it as a gift to Thoas'.

This commerce was the spring of their civilization, and in its service it is believed that they invented the alphabet and were the first to sail by the stars. While other peoples still skirted the coasts, the Phoenicians put out to the open sea, steering their course by the Little Bear; to the north they may have reached the Baltic and the tin pits of Cornwall, and a passage from Herodotus suggests that they rounded the Cape of Good Hope, for some mariners declared that after a long journey down the eastern shore of Africa, the sun had arisen on their right hand. In Mauretania and all the Mediterranean their colonies flourished; their caravanserais stretched beyond Euphrates and in Spain they burrowed through the mines of Tarshish until, it was said, Phoenician captains forged their anchors of silver.

But the backbone of their commerce—the thread of cities between Aradus and Tyre—was constantly menaced. The Phoenicians rarely took to military ventures, and employed mercenaries to fight for them. Theirs was a bourgeois and urban society governed, it is true, by kings, but with the help of a committee of businessmen or a council of elders: cities, as Isaiah claimed, 'whose merchants are princes'.

These towns were gay and worldly places, set comfortably among fields and groves beneath mountains which were thickly wooded. Ancient writers claimed that the Phoenicians were the first to use courtyards in their houses and that they invented music. In their dress they loved bright colours and let their hair fall to their shoulders and barbered their beards thick and pointed: possessors of Tyrian purple and the loveliest glass in the world, drinkers of Damascus wine.

For three centuries after 1200 B.C., while Egypt was dying and Assyria preoccupied, Phoenicia knew a golden age. Sidon had succumbed to the Philistines, who left her in ashes, but Tyre assumed her place and it was not until 814, in the long reign of King Pygmalion, that a dissident body of nobility under

Dido, the king's sister, sailed away to north Africa and founded Carthage. Thereafter Phoenicia was ravaged from the east, and her gifts, including the Great Goddess, began to pass to Greece, until in the Roman period the word 'Phoenician'—which the Greeks had given them, from 'phoinix', 'purple', in admiration of their dyestuffs—had no more ethnic meaning.

In Sidon Phoenician enterprise and animation have left little trace. On the headland the Romans, the Turks and the sea have worn everything away. But inland the orchards, in the rich confinement of their walls, still climb the valley through the musky hills, and here a terrace of huge stones ascends, over-looking the Awali river, the ancient Bostrenus: a temple to Eshmun, Adonis in another guise.

Many questions are posed, for where Adonis is found, there the cult of the Great Goddess is most closely knit with death and with the mystery of rebirth; the Phoenicians, although they inquired little into the broad pattern of existence, adored the goddess, and what is known of her must be largely drawn from them.

The orchards in the valley beneath the temple of Eshmun, and the shining river, attest her basic nature. Water and trees are life. Semites, practical and observant men, did not find her in the mystic heavens but in the earth beneath their feet. She grew in their fields and watered their crops. And the key to this energy was Adonis.

Even in the light of history his origins go back five thousand years to Babylon, where the Sumerians, from an unknown time, worshipped him as the minor deity Tammuz, 'true son of the deep water' and lover of Ishtar, the Great Earth Mother. Every summer he died and Ishtar searched for him in 'the land from which there is no returning'. Then fields and men grew tired. The crops dwindled and the herds died, until Ishtar brought him back to the light. In July, the parched month which the Arabs still call 'Tammuz', the Sumerian women washed and anointed his effigy and mourned his death to the sound of flutes in a dirge which was the knell of all life:

Her lament is for the depth of a garden of trees, where honey
    and wine grow not.
Her lament is for meadows, where no plants grow.
Her lament is for a palace, where length of life grows not.

It was these rites which Semitic tribes brought with them across the Syrian desert long after they had aged in the country of their origin, and which spread along the eastern Mediterranean where the god and goddess assumed many names. Above all in Lebanon the worship of Tammuz ceased to be that of a godling and grew into a national cult, rarefied by religious mysteries; and Ishtar became the Heavenly Goddess, Astarte.

The temple of Eshmun at Sidon tells little of this worship. Its stones betray only a crude power: a stairway for gods, beneath which Roman and Byzantine works lie broken. Excavators and quarrying villagers have cut deep along the wall which upheld the temple against the hill, and uncovered writings on Sidonian history which had been placed there as the secret of the god. A quartet of bulls' heads was discovered in the Roman town, and beneath the terraces, in a chamber awash with the late winter rain, was an empty throne such as often stood in Phoenician shrines, flanked by two lions, emblems of the Mother Goddess. But the most significant pieces came from the Roman city, which inherited the Eshmun worship: statuettes of infant boys, ripe and cherubic, given to the god as pleas for fertility or in gratitude for it. Anemones grew in the classic colonnades, but the temple floor was bare. Behind it an ancient channel carried water through the darkness of the hills to Sidon.

The plan of the sanctuary, although it was huge, and terraced in the Persian fashion, probably reflected hundreds of lesser temples along the foot of the mountains: the rectangular enclosure containing a sacred spring or tree, with a shrine in the centre and an altar before it. The shrine was often empty, but sometimes a statue stood there—an image of the Great Goddess clothed and seated, or a figurine with obtrusive breasts, or simply a phallic stone, a rude assertion of life.

These temples, the high places of the Old Testament, stood on hilltops among trees. On days of ceremony their holy groves were filled with chanting and incense. Votaries brought garlands and libations, emasculate priests performed rites of sacrifice and sacred prostitutes danced for the goddess in the clash of cymbals and had intercourse with strangers. To them all life derived from a single power, and to imitate the workings of this life was magically to strengthen it, so that a Phoenician woman, surrendering herself to an unknown man, gave Astarte power on earth, and eased the return of Tammuz from the grave.

The early Christian attitude to these rites was uncompromising, and the tone of comments has changed little since. 'It is

[7]

probably impossible for one in our day to imagine the depth of immorality and abominable licentiousness which was inwrought in the very spirit and fibre of the old Phoenician Baal-worship.' But our morality is wedded to Christian ethic, and it is hard to understand, in an overcrowded age, the importance of fertility to early peoples. The Phoenicians, who used their brains in commerce, were unable to apply them to the unknown; here they preserved a child's wonder; their gods were elemental and would not indulge in the caprices of Greek and Roman gods. In their daily lives the Phoenicians were probably individual and emotional, as are the Arabs today, but before the gods they saw themselves small. Beneath the surface there was always mystery; the holy statues sweated and groaned; priest-esses grew delirious with dancing, and uttered oracles in the voices of doves or bees.

Yet between men and the goddess the link was fundamental. When they sacrificed to her they not only asked protection for the future but held communion by eating at her altar. They partook of the divine life. And because the goddess was an impartial mother, they thereby acknowledged their kinship with animals and plants as fruit of the earth.

Tacitus tells a story of the emperor Vespasian who, accustomed to the gilded temples of the Palatine, ascended Mount Carmel to consult its Phoenician oracle. He was astonished to find only an altar, set among trees, under the open sky.

*   *   *

It was in a street near the harbour that I met Mahmoud, who liked to tell people about the Castle of the Sea. What he said was scarcely ever accurate, but he repeated it many times, and it took on a timeless flavour. Everybody laughed at Mahmoud. Perhaps it was his strange appearance, for he was very thick-set and had been shot in the thigh while fighting against the Germans at Tobruk so that he walked with the aid of a bamboo stick in a jerky, splayed stride. This gave him a stunted look, and in his heavy face the nose was broken.

He asked me to his home, and I stayed with him for my time in Sidon. He lived in an abandoned prison which had been built by the Ottoman Turks several centuries before. Its entrance led from a bazaar near the harbour—a stairway where torches must have burnt in sconces once, now worn and blemished and opening onto a courtyard where five refugee families from Palestine lived in huts along the walls, or in the cells.

He had a tall room with a tiny window far out of reach. By looking up at the window and seeing where the speck of sunlight fell on the room, he could tell the time of day. In the winter rains the cell, with its thick walls, was one of the few dry places in old Sidon. The bottom of the door had rotted away, but Mahmoud said the rats would not come in because 'Cats stand sentry on the stairway at night; all will be well . . .' Around the room were photographs of ships, for ships were to Mahmoud what cars are to other men. He had worked in the docks in Palestine but had felt friendless and had left when his father died ten years before.

The government had granted him, as a refugee, the prison-room in Sidon, and this, with a television set, supplied all his needs. The set, covered with an embroidered cloth, was enshrined on a small table and was switched on the instant he entered the room. On it sat a lesser tyrant—a Japanese radio—which would fill his silence in the morning; he would twiddle knobs until, for my benefit, he found the B.B.C. World Service, and would listen enraptured to the London Stock Market prices, which he did not understand and which I did not want to hear. But the radio was only the television's shadow. 'Four T.V. channels!' he said each evening, yet only one of them seemed to work, and every few minutes the screen was convulsed by ghosts with elongated jaws and simian foreheads. Mahmoud never noticed. He would sit hunched on the floor, which was covered in reed matting, and shout 'Look, a schooner!' or 'Look, a barge!' and occasionally 'Ah! A dancer!' For Arabic singing and dancing was his other love, and the fulsome figures of the dancers inflamed him.

In the daytime he sometimes worked as a watchman at a factory, but often he would walk round the castle or find his way to the oil refinery a few miles south, where the pipeline reached the sea from Saudi Arabia. There he would watch the ships sucking in oil, like contented sea-elephants.

He showed me round old Sidon: the sweetmakers of the Khan el Saboun, and a mosque whose walls were flaking away in pale heaps, where blossom and nettles grew. And Miyumiye lost among hills—a village of refugees, who looked at us with betrayed faces, and smiled. This was Mahmoud's hospitality. He was always saying in English 'You are my guts' by which, I think, he meant 'guest'; but after a while his resolve would break

[9]

down and he would suggest that we go to the refinery and look at the ships. He knew each one's nationality by its colour.

'Look, two Spanish tankers! Japanese-built. And the one further out is an American; they use Italian crews and pay them less.'

We went to a palace of the great Jumblatt family, which stood on the hill behind Sidon: a baroque mansion in the decadent style of Constantinople. The predatory lions of the Jumblatts were carved over its gateway, and on the house, bolstered by ancient columns, were lions holding garlands—motifs from Roman sarcophagi. The garden was desolate and intoxicating, with dark fir trees framing a far sea, and wild irises beneath the date palms. From it we could see all Sidon in a lake of orchards. I looked north to the promontory of Nebi Yunes, where Moslems believe Jonah to have been disgorged by the whale. Mahmoud looked south to the tankers. 'Beautiful,' he said.

The North Harbour of Sidon is now silted up by the Nile slip-stream and can only be used by small craft. Shielded by a natural reef which was built up and fortified, the Phoenicians sailed here with the spices and pearls of India, Chinese silks and the incense traffic of the Arabian coast. To Egypt they brought cedar-wood and wine and asphalt for embalments, and to the Mediterranean and beyond shipped the produce of Syria and Asia Minor, and Judaean wheat and balm. At first they took squat, horse-headed merchantmen using gaffs and square-sails, but later came penteconters, swift and nervous with fifty oars, and triple-tiered warships with rams and swan's-neck poops, over whose upper decks the soldiers slung their shields.

Today along the North Harbour the boats are hauled up on shore and repitched in spring as in ancient times. Beneath the reef the sea has rubbed away the early mole, but when the waves withdraw a Roman sluice appears, which once let in a current to sweep out the silt that has now throttled the harbour. Ships could reach Sidon in all winds then, for she is surrounded by subsidiary shelters; to the south the slim Egyptian and the Pomegranate harbours, and on the island, oddly wrinkled by the sea, the Foreigner's Port, which was famous in Strabo's day.

The First Crusaders were tempted by such a cluster of anchorages and besieged Sidon under Baldwin I. The city surrendered within seven weeks and the king gave it to Eustace Grenier, lord of Caesarea, as capital of the seignory of Sayette. They built the Castle of St Louis inland on the ruined Phoenician acropolis, but it was destroyed many times and even its containing walls and towers are not original. In 1187 Saladin sacked the city, and after ten years invading knights made their camp-fires of fallen cedar-beams and stabled their horses in the empty halls. Later a garrison of French barons staved off the Saracens from the offshore castle, but the rest of Sidon was ravaged and two thousand people slain.

In 1291 Tyre was abandoned, but at Sidon the Knights Templars moved down from the fortress of St Louis and walled themselves up in the Castle of the Sea. A Mameluke army arrived soon after, and the Templars' Grand Master fled to Cyprus, promising reinforcements, but never returned; and when the Mamelukes began to fill in the narrow channel between the castle and the shore, the Knights, embittered, sailed away to Tortosa.

Sidon has been a Moslem city ever since. Above the Egyptian Harbour the Knights Hospitallers built a church whose walls are now those of the Great Mosque. The Castle of the Sea is a tourist sight and the fortress of St Louis lies in ruins. But opposite is a hill of tiny, serrated shells, a hundred and fifty feet high, woven in goats' tracks and crowned by a cemetery. This is the waste of the Sidonian purple factories, which extracted a colourless fluid from the sea-snail called Murex, and by exposure to the open air and by different treatment in their vats produced the richest dyes in the world.

So popular did the dyed silks become that their export to Rome worried financiers, and Tiberius restricted their use. The spectrum of the 'purple' ran through yellow, green and scarlet, deep wine and the purple of kings, and when the dyeing process was complete the garments did not stain nor fade. I dug my fist into the tight-packed hill and took out a handful of the tiny skeletons. Their secret was said to have been discovered by the Tyrian Adonis, who gave it to Astarte and passed it on to man. But it was common for great discoveries to be attributed to gods. The hill is growing weeds and poppies now, yet the bone-white strata glisten through them: the snail which upset the economy of Imperial Rome.

On my last afternoon at Sidon I sat in Mahmoud's room while he was at the factory. I tried to write letters in its darkness, and was haunted by the tiny window, whose rectangle of light shone high up like an empty frame, once the only star of incarcerated men. Lovelace might have seen a woman in it, Michelangelo set angels to walk there. I, like Mahmoud, used it to tell the time of day, and it had passed from pale to dark blue when there was

[11]

shouting outside and the sound of a man's shoulder at the door. Mahmoud's lock yelped and fell among splinters. In the entrance stood Hassan, a Palestinian refugee who lived downstairs. He was drunk.

'Get out!' he shouted. 'Out! You have no business here! Out!'

I said I was a friend of Mahmoud, but felt a gap growing in my stomach.

He took off his coat and came at me with his fists. Momentarily I wondered about the strength of an Arab. I had not fought anybody since childhood. But his hatred angered me, and I took his wrists, pressing him back to the door, and heaved at him. And to my astonishment his figure dwindled into a star-fish shape on the courtyard floor. Later he ran back and I thought he brought a knife with him, but he only came to collect his coat, and when I saw him I felt ashamed, because he seemed hunched, and much smaller than I, and already in middle age. And a group of women who had gathered outside said that when he had drunk a little arak he became *majnun*, mad.

I tried to mend the door while I waited for Mahmoud's return, wondering if this was how all these people would feel for me once a little drink had washed their *politesse* away. And I was sorry to have brought trouble to Mahmoud, who was a genial, gentle person, and was always saying 'Human beings are only people' or 'People are only human beings.' I felt defeated. You befriend a man, and someone else is angry or jealous. Each friend brings enemies with him. At heart I was feeling guilty because Hassan had perhaps been right. I had no business to be among them.

When Mahmoud came home I told him I must go and that I had disgraced him; but he only smiled. 'You threw him? Good!' I must on no account go. I must stay another night. I was his guts. Just as all the fingers of his hand were of a different length, he said, and each hand deformed by the presence of a thumb, so all people differed, and each nation had its bad members. Hassan, apparently, was the thumb of the Lebanese people.

I was glad I stayed, for the same evening, while walking through the streets with Mahmoud, I met Hassan and smiled at him unhappily, and he ran forward and kissed me on both cheeks. He had drunk too much, he said, and would I forgive him.

When I left the next morning Mahmoud was sad. I would miss a beautiful Swedish tanker which had arrived the evening before, and at breakfast the radio could not be coaxed into relaying Stock Market prices, only his favourite Arabic love songs:

> All people are good
> And were made to love,
> Sometimes at night I dream. . . .

The first day of spring, and the hills are flushed with anemones. Simply to walk through the orchards of Sidon is an intoxication, for it is the month of the orange and lemon harvest. Behind their walls the groves are bent and graceful with fruit. Sometimes the trees are so densely planted that oranges and lemons seem mingled on one bough, and from the oldest trees, whose leaves have fallen, the lemons hang like baubles.

It was probably at this time, on the birth of the new year, that the Phoenicians mourned the passing of Adonis and rejoiced again at his return. All along the coast the effigies of the god, dressed as corpses for burial, were carried in procession and thrown into the springs or out to sea. Women wept and tore their breasts as if their own sons were dead, until a new day dawned and they said that the god had come again. Once a year the people of Sidon still dress as Phoenicians, launch galleys into the North Harbour and sail out past the Castle of the Sea; then, with a sudden purpose and unity, they circle the offshore island where, it is said, a temple once stood to the Tyrian Adonis.

The festivals of spring are given meaning by a tumult of wildflowers over the hills. The Phoenicians must have watched this rebirth, and feeling that the life of plants and humans was almost one, would have seen their own hope in the new flowers. Little is known about their attitude to death and resurrection, because they left few writings behind them. A people to whom life was earnest and immediate may have kept only a dim view of the hereafter, and archaeologists, rummaging among their tombs, decided that they anticipated only a vegetable existence after death, a world of shadows and silence.

If this is so, the powers of the goddess were stunted and the search for her is wasted. But those tombs least exposed to foreign influence, and dating as far back as 2000 B.C., contain people surrounded already by bone utensils and bronze weapons, the paraphernalia of life. Sunk beneath the ground in a bread-oven recess closed by a rock, a man was found with his head resting on a stone, an amethyst necklace at his chin, a gold ring on his finger; beside him was a bronze dagger and a blue faience vase, with perfume.

[13]

Later, stepless shafts were sunk to rooms called 'houses of eternity' and men were buried in plain marble sarcophagi whose lids curved upward in a ridge: fine and simple as a tomb should be. The necropolis of the Sidonian kings, discovered in the orchards more than a hundred years ago, contained many such graves. Generations of the merchant-princes were entombed there and perhaps it answers most nearly the question of the Phoenician after-life, though it is half sealed up and its artefacts dispersed among museums.

The first to be found were anthropoid sarcophagi like those of Egypt. The tomb of Eshmunazar was massive and basalt, scarcely shaped to the form of the body, and carved with a face of bland peace. His inscription warned posterity not to disturb his grave, for 'I am Eshmunazar, king of the Sidonians; son of Tabnit, king of the Sidonians; grandson of Eshmunazar, king of the Sidonians; and my mother, Immiastoreth, priestess of Astarte, our sovereign queen.'

The casket of Tabnit, his father, was discovered soon after in a sunken chamber where tall bronze torches stood, and the withered king still lay inside it, bound to a sycamore plank. Carved near the foot of the sarcophagus, below a kneeling goddess, was the hieroglyphic inscription of an Egyptian general who had occupied the coffin centuries before and had been ejected. The Phoenician engravers began to inscribe king Tabnit's memorial on the head of the stone, but they ran out of space and started again lower down. Tabnit, it seems, married his sister Immiastoreth after the Egyptian fashion, late in the sixth century B.C., and their son Eshmunazar, who perhaps suffered from their union, died childless.

From this time a Hellenistic influence infringes. The vaults were filled with caskets out of whose chilling smoothness gaze stone Greek faces, once lightly coloured. But several tombs were exceptional. In the mausoleum of Sidon stood the marble 'Sarcophagus of Alexander', which may have belonged to the third-century prince Abdolonymos: a tribute to the glory of life, its sides sculptured with the rhythm of hunt and battle, picked out in faded blue and ochre.

Beside it, the 'Tomb of Weeping' was shaped like an Ionic temple, around whose sides eighteen draped women stood in mourning. Mourning for the dead was frowned on by the Greeks and exaggerated by the orientals, but the sarcophagus blended and transmuted their attitudes. In place of the rhythm of the Alexander casket there is austere balance; for masculine pride, domestic dignity and quietude; for the grandeur of life, the sorrow of death. Its restraint and harmony are profoundly touching, and it should surely have belonged to a queen; yet inside was found the well-preserved frame of a man, with two dogs at his feet.

But why did they weep? Because death was extinction or only a parting? The early Phoenicians, with their simple graves, and implements scattered round, anticipated another life in which a man would need his sword and a woman her finery. Then came the Egyptian influence, bringing only the domain of Osiris, passive and sunless, and a passion for the preservation of the body, with its close link to the soul. So the Phoenicians carved curses at the entrances to tombs, denying that any treasure was buried with the dead and asking that their graves be left in peace.

After the fourth century B.C. the shaft tombs disappeared and were replaced with hypogea reached by stairways. Inside were arched recesses in which two coffins might be placed together, and the walls were frescoed with birds and flowers. It became more common for the dead to be buried with their possessions—coins, jewellery, lamps, vases, mirrors. Outside stood many-coloured funerary stelae—bas-relief portraits of the departed, carved with realism, and near the coffin might hang an image of the Great Goddess. Into the Roman period the lead and stone sarcophagi still showed oriental influence, sphinxes and bloated lion masks, and on some reclined the figure of a weeping woman whose prototype, betrayed by the recumbent pose and the uplifting of the left hand, was a famous statue of Aphrodite mourning for Adonis.

So the beliefs of the Phoenicians were mingled with those of other peoples. When asked what hope she holds for men in the hereafter, the goddess grows elusive, and answers teasingly with the voice of Osiris.

3. The Sea Goddess

Aphrodite of the golden toys, see
how after a twelvemonth the Hours
have brought thee back Adonis from
Acheron's ever-flowing stream. . . .
Happy has thy coming found us now,
Adonis, and when thou comest again,
dear will be thy return.

Theocritus

OUR LADY OF MANTARA stands on a hill above the sea. On summer days you may climb to her feet by a stairway round her plinth and look down on Sidon to the north, and to the cloudy Zaharani, 'the River of Flowers', in the south. The Greek Catholic villagers nearby raised her only a few years ago near a rock-cut chapel to the Virgin, which was once a shrine of Astarte. The chapel is scooped from a low, deep cave, and near its apse a vent pierces the rock to the sky; in the Christian shrine the vent is meaningless, but once it may have drawn up the smoke from the altar of the Great Goddess.

There is nothing ironic in the Virgin's presence here. She comes as heiress to an estate already holy. The worship of country people rarely suffers violent change, but is like a house of many periods, and when new stones must be laid they are fitted among the old and buttressed by them.

The olive trees of Mantara, rough and scented against the hill, bear witness to this continuity. Their ancestors were planted by Phoenicians, who brought the first olive tree to Greece, and in their shadow the villagers have lived a life whose blessing was its permanence.

I came here at Easter, which the first Christians perhaps established on the day of the resurrection of Adonis, celebrated in Phoenicia near the Vernal Equinox. The spring followed a freak winter which had brought famine to Syria, and it thundered and hailed over the village until at eight o'clock the people knelt for Mass in the church.

Children wandered between their fathers in the front pews and their mothers who sat behind, and the elders slumped in high-backed chairs against the nave, and occasionally slept. Mass was like a carnival, the women in bright coats, their lace veils drawn back, and boys throwing fire-crackers outside. And once or twice the church bells fraternized with the nasal Arab liturgy, their ropes and pivots snoring like a steamship's engine in the roof.

The communicants were mostly women, and to each the Holy Body, dipped in the Sacred Blood, was administered over a white cloth. It was accepted with folded arms in a ritual which must have seemed more than half occult, dazed by the chandeliers and the priest's white canonicals and sharp incantation, to which the chorus rose like a hum of bees. They left the church to the greeting 'Christ has risen', to which was answered 'He has risen indeed!' as the ancient Romans, at an older feast, hailed each other with the words 'Adonis has risen!'

At midday families fed on the date and walnut cakes called *mahmoul*—very sweet and rich—which are special to Easter, and in the afternoon the children processed around the church with giant candles. Toward sunset the women walked to the grotto of Our Lady of Mantara, where they prayed, without knowing, in the precincts of Astarte, and lit candles to the Holy Mother, writing in the book beside the altar: 'Holy Mother, have pity on us and save us' or 'Mother of Mantara guard my son and give my daughter children.'

St Helena herself is said to have sent the chapel's holy ikon from Constantinople, and the grotto was an established place of worship early in the fourth century, dedicated to 'Our Lady of the Awaiting'; for here, they say, the Virgin waited for Christ when He visited the coasts of Tyre and Sidon.

Not far from the chapel, in another cave, archaeologists had seen the rock carving of a woman. Nobody knew for certain who she was—perhaps Astarte, perhaps the Virgin.

I searched the ground where she had been located, but found nothing. A group of men came to help me, hoping that I might uncover treasure, and soon half the villagers said that they had caves on their land. They showed me pits and grottoes and mere shelves in the rock, and each time I descended, flickering a torch across walls contaminated by tree-roots, they crowded at the entrance, afraid of the dark, and saying that wild animals might live there.

At last, under an overgrown field, we found a rock-cut chamber which must have been the true cave; but it contained only a tiny bat, hanging like a folded tulip, and a hillock of earth where half the ceiling had cascaded in. Perhaps the carving lies beneath it, or had been broken, or carried away to build an olive terrace. Even when she was found she was enigmatic—a figure in faded stone, carved long ago. The Mother who spreads her arms over Lebanon.

*　　*　　*

I turned in the direction of Tyre, twenty-two miles to the south, walking through orchards and along the sea. Tel el Buraq lies between the road and the coast, built of Roman stones, soft with the drip of water from its green springs: perhaps the site of Ornithopolis, 'the City of Birds' mentioned by Strabo. And four miles beyond is Sarafand, once famous as Sarepta for its glass and wines, but now a straggly village. In Crusader times it was handsomely walled, with a Carmelite priory and a castle near the sea; but by the end of the thirteenth century its people had moved inland from a pirate-stricken coast, and made a new town and a peaceful living in the fields.

For several centuries the Crusader ruins were impressive on the shore; but during the last hundred years they were carried off to build Beirut, and the site of the old city is marked now by a white-domed shrine to a forgotten saint. It is supposed to have been built over the ruins of the Crusader church to Elijah, for the first Book of Kings says that at Sarepta the prophet took sanctuary with a widow whom he found gathering sticks at the gate, and raised her son from the dead; but the sanctuary is called 'Weli el Kadr', 'The Shrine of the Great One', and nobody could tell me the Great One's history, except that he had stayed there long ago, as Elijah did, and had gone away.

The coast is still rich in orchards, but its strength has gone, and the cities which lined the sea even in Crusader times have dwindled to poverty. A few miles beyond Sarafand, past seaside restaurants, I reached Adlun, which was perhaps the Mutatio ad Nonum of the Pilgrim of Bordeaux, though nobody knows. In its grey cliffs the Phoenicians dug tombs, which were dank and smelly with rain, and Palaeolithic men lived among its caves and left their chipped tools behind them.

I camped on a hill within sight of the sea, by the spires of wild lilies. In the morning I was awoken by goat-bells among the holm-oaks, and saw herdsmen crouched under their pointed capes in a harsh wind. I was offered breakfast by a lorry-driver's family, whom I remember only as a row of luminous eyes in sallow faces, and four hours later I watched Tyre rising from the sea.

In almost all times but our own Tyre was rich and spirited, and would have remained so had the Roman frontiers held. More reflective cities change, as a new age doubts the ideals of its fathers; so thought may only sustain the era which gave it, then pass subtly into the fibre of accepted things; but commerce is a coarser grain in history and can endure for centuries.

Herodotus says that Tyre was founded in 2750 B.C. on the morning of the Phoenician age, and for three thousand years she did good business. Her traders were 'the honourable of the earth' and the city itself, said Ezekiel, was 'merchant of the people for many isles. . . . Thy borders are in the midst of the seas, thy builders have perfected thy beauty.'

Now Tyre is shrunken on her spit of land: a pink and amber village which has half-slid back into the waves. As I reached the first houses over an arc of sand, even the feeling of a dense and pretty hamlet was dispelled. Tyre merely fell apart, vacuous and shabby.

Once she straddled two islands and was built up on the coast; and Hiram, the Tyrian king who sent craftsmen and cedarwood for the temple of Solomon, filled in the straits between the isles and linked her with a causeway to the shore. But in the end the sea has been the architect of Tyre, has turned the island to a peninsula by pouring sand against the mole which Alexander laid, and has silted up the Sidonian Harbour where only double-masted fishing-boats sail. And the breakwater of the South Harbour, with its towers and battlements, was breathed on by the waves, and vanished.

Between her ruined bays the fallen city spreads among asphodel, retaining in her walls the monolithic stones of Phoenicia, Greek imagination, Roman order and the brown Byzantine roads; but she keeps them carefully, each as a facet of her nature, and still seems to include in her dominion the wide hem of the sea. She has been excavated well and has the air, at first, of a tended garden, with a flowering of crown daisies and geraniums planted in sarcophagi. I followed the paved grey marble of the street which joined the harbours, and saw the granite columns of the decumanus propped against the clouds. To the east are Roman baths, piled with the bricks which were warmed to heat the waters; to the west, white and unfamiliar, a rectangular Hellenistic amphitheatre where international games

Tyre: columns standing and fallen

Tyre: the 19th century view. (From Colonel Sir Charles Wilson: *Picturesque Palestine, Sinai and Egypt*, 1882)

were held every five years. Cisterns lie beneath it, interconnected, their vaults fallen in, and I began to understand how Tyre sustained her sieges, locked in her island walls a hundred and sixty feet high, and owning the sea. Sargon of Assyria raised his siege in 715 after ten years of hopeless blockade, though Sennacherib succeeded in 700 and rendered Tyre too weak to hold her empire. Nebuchadnezzar, after a thirteen-year investment, was forced to conclude a treaty, and Alexander took the city only after seven months, the longest any place withstood him.

The stones glowed after night rain, stones of a city tight-packed and formidable, whose craftsmen left behind their yellow and sea-green glass in circular ovens, whose looms wove Chinese silk and whose dyeing vats, said Strabo, polluted the air and made the town unhealthy. No doubt it was always disordered, though the Greek streets were straight and clean. 'The houses here, it is said, consist of many stories, of more even than Rome', but now it has shuffled the eras together almost beyond analysis, one moment pressing through the grass the marble floors of Byzantium, with crushed glass mosaics and delicate capitals; the next a Roman water-pipe, the gravestone of Greek soldiers, a Phoenician slab on which some Crusader carved a cross of St John. Over all, the steel-grey lizards dawdle with distended bellies, bull-frogs mate in the marshes beyond the Roman baths and from a long way away sounds the voice of a guide to a line of tourists: 'Please come this way and do not touch the objects. . . . The principal god of Tyre was Melqart or Moloch, famous for his sacrifices of small children. . . .' And the tourists, who have been pestered for money by small children all afternoon, trail away mutely over the stones.

Melqart was brother to the Sidonian Eshmun, and both were variants of Adonis; but long before classical times these child-devouring gods had grown away from the early image of the Babylonian youth. While the Greeks recognized Adonis in the cults of northern Lebanon, they associated Eshmun with Aesculapius, god of healing, and identified Melqart with Heracles, whose twelve labours were perhaps based on the feats of Phoenician sailors.

The Greeks came like sunlight on the Levant. Just as the sudden order of their columns transforms Phoenician towns even in ruin, so the clear light of their intelligence brings a new understanding of the Great Goddess and of Adonis.

Astarte came to Greece by stages, stayed at Cyprus many years and absorbed the worship of Ariadne there. Perhaps because Phoenician merchants brought her over the ocean, the legend grew that she was born of foam and came in a seashell to Cytherea beyond the coast of Sparta. A king, it was said, jnstalled her cult in Athens so she might bless him with children, and the Greeks accepted her and called her Aphrodite.

Except in Corinth, always quick to receive oriental influence, her rites were purified, and to her basic quality as divinity of earth were added others. Her name was given to bays and promontories, and her temples stood high above the sea, where traders and fishermen invoked her against shipwreck, naming her at Cnidus 'the goddess of fair winds' or at Troezen 'the watcher from the cliffs'. In Sparta and Cyprus she was martial; she became the wife of the war god, Ares. And because her generative powers were closely linked with death, she was called at Argos 'the goddess of the graves', and at Delphi presided over libations to the dead.

Yet primarily she grew to be a divinity of love, the most gentle and female of the goddesses: 'Aphrodite of the side-long glance', 'laughter-loving Aphrodite', 'Aphrodite of the whispering voice'. And when in *The Iliad* she lifts her wounded son Aeneas from the spear-tip of Diomedes, the Greek 'realizing that this was some timid goddess' pursued her and cut her in the hand. ' "Daughter of Zeus", he cried. "Be off from this battle and leave war alone. Is it not enough for you to set your snares for feeble womenfolk?" '

So by Homer's time she was already Hellenized, the child of Zeus by the nymph Dione. Law and ethics were beyond her sphere, for she dealt with those things over which men held scant control: the flux of the year, the vale of shadows, the caprices of human love. Her train was made up of joy and instinct—the Charities, who own the flowers of spring; wanton Eros and the Horae, bringers of the new season. And her supplicants must above all have been the childless and the lovelorn, who saw her close and human, as Sappho did:

> Eternal Aphrodite, of the long tresses, child of Zeus,
>   on your rainbow-dappled throne,
>   I beseech you,
>
> Leave me not in sorrow and bitter
>   anguish of soul to suffer,
>   dear Lady,
>
> But come to me, if ever in the past, at other times,
>   you hearkened to my songs,

and harnessed the golden chariot, and left
your father's house and came to me. . . .

Beside the written word, the goddess may be traced in stone.
From the Phoenicians the classical world inherited a draped,
oriental figure and a heavy-breasted symbol of fecundity. These
the Greeks, who first gave dignity to man, took and altered out
of recognition. Astarte became ancestress to some of the loveliest statues of antiquity. She was the first whom the Greek
sculptors carved naked, and they raised her from the realm of
vegetable faith to an emblem of beauty and humanity.

But as she became more human, so she grew less godlike, in
character as in stone. For a moment in the lives of some cities,
or even of some men, faith and reason may be well blended.
Astarte, goddess of faith, lends divine energy and humility.
Aphrodite grants imagination and the range of human feeling.
Without Astarte she is aimless; Astarte without her is mere
instinct; one the playing of a flute, the other the clash of a
cymbal.

This moment of balance, if it ever existed, is echoed by the
Aphrodite of Praxiteles, a portrait of Phryne, his beloved, which
stood in an open temple above the sea on the island of Cnidus.
'The finest statue not only of Praxiteles, but of the whole world',
wrote Pliny, and even from the copies which remain, one may
believe him. The goddess is portrayed probably stepping into a
pool, and with her left hand discards her robe. Hellenic poise and
majesty give grace to her movement, and she accepts without
shame her heavy and desirable body.

The Venuses which came after—the fruitful beauty of the
Capitoline, the startled Medici—never shared this naturalness.
They cover themselves. The cosmic view of love and fertility is
corrupted. It was not long before the cult of the goddess grew
over-sweet. Prostitutes regarded her as their patron, and
Philetaerus, exaggerating, still wrote that: 'It is not for nothing
that everywhere there are temples of Aphrodite the mistress,
but nowhere shrines of Aphrodite the married goddess.' So the
last worshippers of Astarte mimicked the devotions of the first,
and were taken out of the hand of God.

*   *   *

The southern harbour of Tyre is deserted—a beach where columns lie half-submerged. At evening fishermen edge into the waves as if to attack the sea and suddenly throw their nets. The mediaeval traveller Benjamin of Tudela said that Tyre had been inundated and that 'whoever sails may observe the towers, the markets, the streets and the halls at the bottom of the sea'. But this is no longer true, only here and there the remains of the harbour works show darkly under the waves.

I spread my sleeping-bag on the sand, hoping that Murex shells would dye it purple by morning, and watched the sun go down stormily and leave its colours in the sea. A fisherman lit a fire on the beach, and I awoke much later to silence, and the waves frosty under the moon.

I looked out to the southern cliffs—the Promontarium Album of Pliny—where Alexander cut a road and raised a fortress against Tyre. The moon was so bright that I read how he took the city, in the history of Arrian. In his day Tyre was a fortified isle and while he constructed a mole from the mainland the Tyrians shot his workmen, burnt his protective towers, mined the sea with stones and used divers to cut loose his ships. But with ballistas mounted on boats Alexander breached the southern ramparts, and ringed the city with triremes. 'The ships were no sooner under the wall and the ladders fixed than the Long-shields, with Admetus in the fore, mounted them and pressed valiantly into the breach; and soon Alexander himself came to his support and was fighting in the thick of battle . . .' Meanwhile the Tyrian fleet was rammed in the southern harbour, now glassy with moonlight, and the city fell, leaving eight thousand dead in its streets.

In time Alexander's mole silted up and turned the island into a headland. The Romans closed its neck with fortifications and paved a road into the city through an avenue of tombs, piercing the walls under a triumphal gate. The tombs are still there, the family mausolea desecrated, and bones are heaped in sarco-phagi, white from fifteen centuries of darkness; the skulls of Byzantine children. And the triumphal arch is there too, hand-some in its simplicity, uncoarsened by the triumph which raised it.

From here in early morning I walked through fields of asters and pale cyclamen to look for Paleotyrus—old Tyre—which stood on the mainland and was abandoned in the time of Alexander, who built his breakwater with its stones. Its site is occupied by Reshidiye, a village of refugees, and only the springs of Ras el Ain, which the earliest Phoenicians enclosed nearby, suggest that it existed.

The springs are still encased in stone, raised high above ground level, and their water is borne on arches across the plain to Reshidiye. The Assyrians, unable to capture Tyre, left guards here for five years, forcing the citizens to drink from wells inside the town, but the memory of their loutishness is gone, and the city survived.

Midway between old and new Tyre is the village of Tel Maashuq, piled against a hill as if by accident under the tombs of Moslem saints. Pitted with shafts, it was once the site of a temple where the waters of Ras el Ain were diverted to island Tyre. Maashuq means 'the lover' or 'beloved' and the acropolis was probably sacred, under some guise, to Adonis, but is smothered now.

Barely a mile to the east, grottoes were sunk for burial in the cliffs of El Awatim in Roman years. I plunged from one to another through screens of giant clover, and wondered what the advent of the Greeks and Romans had done to explain the life beyond the grave. Only one tomb, whose stucco walls were taken to the Beirut Museum, offered any answer. Its frescoes are of Greek myths—gods and men now darkened or faded, but infused with pastoral grace: Achilles, with godlike condescension, permitting the aged Priam to kiss his hand; Tantalus who stole nectar for men; Persephone borne in Pluto's chariot to the underworld. But the most poignant is an assertion of redemption in which Heracles, the Tyrian Adonis, full of strength and mildness, extends a hand to the austere shade of Alcestis, and leads her back to the light.

The link with Phoenicia is fragile, but present; the idea of futurity ill-formed, but the concept of resurrection strong. The Elysian Fields may have seemed remote, even undesirable, but it was not in despair that the Tyrians wended along the funerary path from the villas and warehouses of the plain, and sealed up their dead in the dark, fragrant hills.

Even the Adonis myth was Hellenized. The Phoenicians, assuming that all men knew the story, left scarcely a word of it in writing, but Greek historians crystallized and adorned it. Tammuz, the corn-spirit, became the graceful shepherd Adonis (from the Semitic 'Adon', 'lord') and Aphrodite hid him in a chest while he was a child and placed him in the care of Persephone, queen of the shadows. But she, seeing his beauty, refused to give him back, though Aphrodite came to hell to fetch him, so Zeus decreed that Adonis would live half the year with Aphrodite in the world of light and half in the dark regions. Then Aphrodite's husband, Ares god of war, transformed himself into a wild boar and killed Adonis while he hunted, and from the youth's blood and the tears of the goddess sprang the crimson anemone, which is scattered over the hills in spring but whose petals flake away in the violence of the wind.* Yet the judgement of Zeus remained unaltered, and the Greek myth, like the Babylonian, saw Adonis rise each year in the triumph of love over death.

The ancient writers gave many versions of the legend, which they linked with Cyprus, the first Phoenician colony. The Cypriot king Pygmalion fell in love with a statue of the Great Goddess and took it to his bed, and Cinyras, who came after him, wedded his own daughter Myrrha and became the father of Adonis. Myrrha, in shame, asked to be changed into something neither living nor dead, lest she shed a curse on either world, and the gods, taking pity on her, turned her into the myrrh tree. But Apollodorus wrote that Adonis was born of this tree and was killed by the anger of Artemis.

In Cyprus alone the legends varied, and some islanders believed that the goddess had thrown herself over the Leucadian rock in despair, and showed her grave there. Frazer in *The Golden Bough* says that the name of the goddess is retained in some parts of Cyprus 'for in more than one chapel the Cypriote peasants adore the mother of Christ under the title of Panaghia Aphroditessa'.

Wherever the cult of Adonis followed that of Aphrodite it helped preserve her nature as a mother goddess; but its dancing-girls and eunuch priests—the religion of instinct and inspiration—were offensive to rational men, and it is not before the fifth century that the worship is mentioned in Athens, by the poet Cratinus, who describes a playwright as unfit 'to train a chorus even for the Adonis-festival'. At first sight it is strange that the cult survived at all in the temperate, masculine climate of Greece, and Lucian doubtless spoke the mind of his Hellenized contemporaries when he called it 'the lascivious orgy over the shepherd; the secret rites of initiation, the disreputable mysteries from which men are excluded . . . mere corruption of the mind'. But the Peloponnesian War, breaking in fragments a world which had seemed ordered, eased its advance, and

* The Arabs still call the anemone 'the Wounds of Naaman', or 'darling', which was an epithet of Adonis.

Plutarch wrote that when the Athenian army was embarking for its disastrous expedition against Syracuse, it was the day of the Adonia, and the streets were lined with effigies of corpses laid on biers, where women wailed and struck their breasts.

Sitting below the tombs of El Awatim, sleepy with clover and the sun on the cliffs, it seemed that the gods had, after all, vanished with the ancients, senselessly worshipped or treated as merely human. One might understand their past, but it fell short of the present. When the anemones flowered there was no informing spirit in them. The leaves which brushed my hand were numb. The life of a man or a plant was a chance cluster of molecules, a moment of spray on a calm sea. . . .

I heard a voice above me. A man was standing on the cliffs, a policeman angry and self-important. He shouted at me to come up, and a group of villagers appeared among the trees and watched us indifferently.

He had decided that I was a spy for Israel and told me so. What else would one be doing hunting through grottoes in the middle of the afternoon? Later, sitting in the police station, he sifted through my pack, looking for maps. He found a small-scale plan of the 'Temple of Bacchus' at Baalbec, which might have been a military area, and some code-like Greek inscriptions. Did I really expect him to believe that I was in those caves for pleasure?

He asked me to read out my notes to him. I started with the tale of how Zeus had abducted Europa from the shores of Tyre, then wove my way among historical jottings, omitting the deeds of the Hebrew kings and Ezekiel's curse on Sidon. The policeman softened a little but made me empty the rest of my pack. Among the papers which fell out were some old French military maps, very detailed, and covering the more difficult mountain terrain. I watched his hands pick up and discard the papers which had fallen on top of them: vaccination certificates, a diary and a letter from my father telling me to take care. But a sergeant came in, and as the policeman looked up I slid the maps back under the pack. When he resumed his inspection it was to pick up a pamphlet which read 'Come to sunny Lebanon, where the people will everywhere greet you with a smile. . . .'

By this time he was wilting. He offered me coffee which I refused with dignity, and ended by saying that he was miserable about his mistake, that I was very kind and *helou*, sweet, and that he was coming to England soon and would look out for me.

[27]

Shorn of his chance of promotion, he left me for his duties in the village while I, feeling dishonest and a little smug, started back towards Tyre.

Somewhere along my way were the fortifications of the Crusaders, dimples under the sand, but I could not identify them. William of Tyre, who was elected its archbishop in 1173, described the city as defended on the sea side by a double rampart, and 'on the east, where the approach by land lies, it has a triple wall, with enormously high and massive towers so close together that they almost touch one another. There was a broad mole also, through which the citizens could easily let in the sea from both sides.' The Crusaders took Tyre only by starving it, then held it for a hundred and sixty years. Conrad of Montferrat twice repulsed Saladin from its gates, and the Moslems never captured the city, but found it abandoned after the fall of Acre and levelled it into the sand.

One could forget that Tyre had belonged to the knights were it not for the Venetian cathedral. Like a galleon foundered in a sea of stones, it has yet the appearance of suspension, of enduring a lull in the storm of its decay. Rose-granite columns breathe warmth through the ruin, and a marble-pillared transept stands in the west where the foundations of the triple apse make gaunt arcs in the grass.

A Byzantine basilica stood on the site once—the finest church in Phoenicia, lavish in its workmanship. Eusebius delivered the oration at its consecration, rather pompously, and Origen, who died at Tyre in about 254, was supposed to have been buried there. The Venetians built their cathedral from these stones and dedicated it to St Mark; and when Frederick Barbarossa led the Third Crusade through Cilicia and was drowned in the Calycadnus, his knights rode down the long coast to the Tyrian cathedral and buried the bones of the warrior-king within the confines of the Holy Land.

Soon after the Moslem sack of Tyre, Abulfeda described it as desolate. For four centuries only a few fishing families lived in its vaults, and Isaiah's prophecy was fulfilled: 'It shall be a place for the spreading of nets in the midst of the sea.' In 1766 Metawileh tribes began to rebuild Tyre, and still inhabit it. They exported a little cotton and tobacco, and supplied a market for charcoal-burners who came down from the hills. But Djezzar Pasha took away whole sections of the town to rebuild Acre, and even in the nineteenth century the biblical scholar Edward Robinson described the Crusader cathedral as 'wholly filled up by the mean hovels of the city; many of which are attached, like swallows' nests, to its walls and buttresses'.

Now the port is stifled and empty. The closed Israeli border has left it in a commercial cul-de-sac, a testimony to the voice of the prophet and the might of the sea. And when I walked among the older ruins, supine on their forelock of land, they too seemed no longer to desire life, nor to give their suffering stones to any new Phoenicia.

4. A Faded King

There is a generation, whose teeth
are as swords . . .

Proverbs xxx. 14

THE AQRAB RIVER VALLEY might have been scooped out
by man, so regular and polished are the stairways of its stone,
and so smooth the crescents it describes. Wildflowers crowd the
steepness of its banks, careless of where they grow, and shine
among the rocks; and at last, because they became too dense and
delicate to walk through, I sat down among them and cooled my
feet in the water.

The sea was only five miles behind, but it was two months
before I reached it again. A long way to the north the mountains
left their summits ghostly in the sky. I planned to walk through
them in a long arc, following the cleft of the Nahr el Litani, the
Leontes river of the Greeks, into the Druse hills. Higher still,
leaving behind the palaces of Lebanon's mountain kings, I hoped
to cross the peaks of Sannin in May, and come down through
country bright with rivers, tracing the ancient Lycus to the sea.

But first there were the hills in the south, the only part of
Lebanon in which I did not care to walk. Half the area is a
military zone bordering Israel and is inhabited by Metawilleh, dissenting Moslems whom past travellers noted for their
toughness and treachery. Yet already I was inside their territory, with Israel less than ten miles to the south; farmers were
bent in static labour on the slopes above, and the land was
deep in flowers. Along the crown of the hill, called Hanaouch,
the Phoenicians had a citadel, and dug tombs which were never
filled. The rock-cut shelves where their buildings stood, and the
steps which they carved, are still new in the stone, and a
charcoal-burner, digging up a dead tree-root nearby, discovered
a complete set of ancient funerary glass. Many such villages
must once have lined these mild hills and rivers, and flourished
within the orbit of Tyre. Even in the day of Pliny, who is here
cursory but accurate, the dominion of the mother-city stretched
nineteen miles to her south.

Near to Hanaouch a sepulchre is raised on three tiers of stones.

High in its casket the plunderers tore a hole and pulled the body out, leaving a grey cenotaph to an unknown king. Underneath, a shaft plunges to a cavern, older than the tomb, and there are Phoenician walls and grottoes and a cistern sealed with plants. Tradition says that the grave was that of Hiram, ruler of Tyre and friend of Solomon, but for this there is no foundation. Probably it was raised five centuries later during the empire of the Persians, who built such tombs, and belonged to a governor on Tyre's eastern frontier, or a lord of Abarnahara.

In those times it glorified life, standing as monument to a man's past renown beside the roadway from Tyre to Damascus. But now, its soul plucked out, it utters only the desire to be remembered, and the failure. Men thought more of reputation then. To live on in the minds of others was a resurrection solid and worth dying for. 'It is a lovely thing to live with courage, and to die, leaving behind an everlasting renown', and a man might build his tomb against the sky, as if life could stare out death; though this was not the Phoenician way.

I planned to spend the night under the olive trees above the river. The ground was musky with asphodel, and the last shepherds were taking away their destructive goats like black beetles between the hills. But some farmers came out from the hamlet of Ain Baal, whose name and a few columns remembered a Phoenician sanctuary there, and they persuaded me back to their village, arguing over who should be my host.

They were the first Metawilleh with whom I stayed. We sat in a two-roomed hut whose walls were of mud, with a corrugated iron roof which pattered under rain all night. There was a single bed, where a hazel-eyed girl moaned and clasped her forehead, and a shelf with a jar of artificial flowers which the Arabs love, even when surrounded by real ones. The family was called Bedawi—immemorial name—and instead of speaking, the men shouted, as the Bedawi do, wanting to know what I was doing and why I walked when foreigners could always pay for taxis. They were dark and thick-set, like boxers. The young men bellowed and laughed impulsively, but their eyes were mirrored in those of their fathers, where they had grown quiet and flinty.

Through a crack in the door came the stifled giggling of Madonna-eyed girls, and the women dropped their headscarves from their mouths to stare at me, flashing gold teeth. The mother of all these children said: 'Your parents must be afraid for you. They must wonder when you will come home.' She looked at me a long time, her face creased as a rock is by water, and smiled slowly. She was, perhaps, the only person there able to imagine her own suffering in the body of another.

The men's voices were so harsh that my understanding of Arabic, already poor, almost vanished. They could not comprehend this, only talked louder and with fiercer emphasis, and nudged me at each sentence, as if brute noise would break through to my mind. Why did I walk when I could drive? Why come to Tyre when Beirut was bigger? What was the point of the Phoenicians and Crusaders? They were dead. How much had I paid for my boots, my pack, my watch? And a swarthy youth asked me to send him money from England, repeating his name and address many times. 'Fifteen pounds, you understand? *English* pounds, not Lebanese. All you have to do is put them in an envelope and send them to this address. . . .'

I wanted to like them. Not long ago a Metawilleh would not eat with a stranger. He might let a Christian drink from one of his earthen vessels, but he would break it immediately after. Now some women came in carrying trays of rice and *markouk* bread in their blunt, farmer's hands, and we ate hard, because it was late and cold. Afterwards the sick girl was ordered out of the bed and it was given to me, and when I passed her some aspirin it only drew theatrical tears.

At night a palsied glow filled the room from a green bulb in the ceiling—darkness is feared—and after a few minutes the youth came over and nudged me. The Phoenicians and Crusaders were gone, he said, but he was alive. Did I understand that I was to send him fifteen pounds from England in an envelope? Here was the address again. . . . He took up my socks, which smelt, and thrust them back and forth between us in an act of giving, to clarify his idea. I nodded and turned over, and he nudged me again and repeated that the Phoenicians and the Crusaders were dead, but . . .

I lay awake a long time, listening to cats crying in the night like lost babies. A distorting mirror lined one wall of the room and in it I saw sleeping men humped morgue-like on the green-lit floor. The Metawilleh are poorer than other Moslems, perhaps because they migrated only recently to southern Lebanon from the east; perhaps because their religion nurtures them in hatred and estrangement. Their name means 'Friends of Ali', and they are members of the great Shiite sect which dominates Iran and Iraq and which does not acknowledge the early caliphs but believes in the sanctity of a line of imams stemming from Ali, Mahomet's son-in-law. In Lebanon there

[33]

are other groups, occupying Tyre and Sidon and the Beqaa valley, and wherever they live they seem to bring poverty with them.

I am at my least forgiving in the early morning, and it was very early when the youth nudged me again and there was an argument among the men about something I could not understand. I remained in the bed, irritated that this fury could continue in a world of goats and flowers, and wondered if such unhappiness was not a sneer at nature, and why the new day dawned at all. Then the hazel-eyed girl came in and smiled at me because her headache had cleared, and eventually I said good-bye and tried to thank them.

As I walked down to the river, wildflowers covered the roughness of the valley. In all the hills, too steep for trees, they seemed to be the only life: tordylion like broken snowflakes and the wide-open flax, with bugloss underfoot, royal purple veined in pink; and in and out of rocks the violet anemones and scarlet ones, Adonis blood, with campions and the dark corn poppy. The river led along cliffs beneath Kana, with its mosques and Greek Catholic church grouped indulgently together on the hill. My first Lebanese snake was sleeping on a rock eight miles from the Israeli border, where a blanket of cranesbill turned the stones to pink. I scrambled to a track and it was not long before the postman from Kana came skimming through the dust on his motor-scooter. A ride was obligatory. I thought I was going to die. We moved airborne down the hill, twisted between shrubs and swam among the rocks. The track was merely a line to which we might return when we were lost. 'It's a good life, a postman's!' he shouted over his shoulder, and leapt a furrow. 'I know girls in every village!' We spun through drifts of cyclamen, crushing the surprised and windswept faces, groaned up a hill of garbled stones, down again, chased a lizard through the broom and found the track.

He dropped me in a valley near the village of El Mezraa, where high on a ravine I saw a plaque, an Egyptian carving of the kind which goes unnoticed in the temple-fields of Karnak, but which appeared with strangeness on the Phoenician hill. Four stepped bands were cut around it and it had been indented two feet in the cliff and so preserved. Above spread the winged globe and uraeus, and beneath were divinities who seemed to have half crept back into the rock. A figure standing on a plinth held up something vanished, and a faded king was seated on a throne in the onion headdress of Osiris; before him, cast almost from a change in the stone colour, two worshippers approached, and I thought I saw the rounded head of Horus the falcon, or of the goddess Isis. Tempered by the winds and the sun, the carvings might have grown with the mysterious hill, a pattern formed by nature of the elemental gods. Perhaps they were left as a prayer by some Egyptian king marching north against the Hittites, or carved by southern-influenced Phoenicians; but what they had meant to say, chipping at the mountain for so many days, was of importance always: the king they carved was Osiris, the child of earth god and sky goddess, and husband to Isis, 'Creator of Green Things'. In his primal state he was a deity of fruit and harvest, who was slain by his brother and floated out to sea in a wooden chest until he came to Byblos on the shore of Lebanon. Here the erica-tree grew up around his coffin and the ruler of the land took it as a pillar for his palace. But Isis found it and carried the body back to Egypt, and after many troubles restored the god to life. So he became lord of the underworld, whose heaven was a country of high corn and fresh rivers.

The Egyptians buried images of Osiris, stuffed with corn at the time of sowing, and took such figures with them to the grave as surety for resurrection. In some towns the Phoenicians worshipped him with Adonis, for both were deities of vegetation, whose passing and return were celebrated with lament and rapture. And so Osiris is his brother, an image faint on the rock, but the needs which gave him birth still poignant and unanswered.

For a short while I walked on, aware of the closeness of the military zone and buffeted by every wave of the land, a begging woman disquieting me in one valley, a peasant's rich smile and the scent of fallen lemons pleasing me in the next. Soon afterwards I set my compass for the hamlet of Joweiya five miles to the north, and walked across the hills. They were fallow, but handsome as old peasants are, veins of rugged stone about them and a bristle of holm-oaks. Every time I reached a ridge I saw the sea, and below in empty valleys the barley shimmered, as if a god breathed there, and hawks hung on the wind.

Joweiya was pretty, and I was taken in for the night by a mother-figure, calm and billowing, who plied me with oranges and medlars and gave me a huge bed. 'I open my heart to you,' she said, throwing back her thin veil. And she did. Her husband was wizened and puckish, weathered honey-brown. He had been a butcher in the Argentine for fifteen years, littered his talk with

Spanish and danced for me with imaginary castanets, his narrow shoulders bent and the turban round his fez flying out.

They had two sons away in Africa, and two daughters, one of whom still lived with them. Noha had fine black hair and a slim figure, but five years before, when almost a woman, a gas stove had exploded over her. Now her whole face seemed incompletely moulded, pulled by grafted skin into troughs and ridges, and when she smiled she seemed to split apart. Yet underneath, the bones were beautiful, broad and regular; her mouth, tugged up at one corner by the startled flesh, had been sweet and full, and there was still a radiance about her, as if some early pride had left its aura. Her married sister had the same bird-like nose, but her face was clear and silken as if Noha's pain, by some atrocious magic, had left her ageless.

Joweiya was an empty village. People came and went like migratory birds. Most of the men worked in other towns and every family had a relative abroad, emigrated to West Africa or South America. In mediaeval times the men were itinerant tinkers and the women gave themselves freely to strangers who came to the village—a left-over, perhaps, from the Adonis festivals. But although Joweiya is ancient, with Phoenician cisterns, its people are Metawilleh who came not long ago, and the many kinds of face which I saw—negroid, Turkish, even a pure Castilian doña—were the fruit of foreign wives brought back by émigrés.

I had a room by a terrace overlooking the village, and a garden where geraniums were trying to grow. On one wall hung a tapestry of Venetian ladies buying parakeets in the Piazzetta San Marco; on another a picture of the Virgin cradling the Holy Child, for the Moslems reverence Christian figures.

The old man left at dawn for the slaughterhouse, where he cut the animals at the throat, as a Moslem must, to let the blood out cleanly. And I said good-bye, while Noha turned her sad face squarely to me, thrusting a pen into my hands, and asked me to write to them.

* * *

Every hill is crowned by a village, a saint's tomb, a castle or a convent; but beyond Joweiya the country changed. The ridges drooped and darkened, and the road was blocked by soldiers, stern in helmets with camouflage nets, behind sodden heaps of sandbags.

'You are entering a forbidden area.'

I had a four-day military permit from Beirut, acquired with difficulty, and a letter from the Ministry of Tourism. They let me go, but looked at me, I thought, as sportsmen watch grouse out of season.

A hailstorm crept over my shoulder while I was walking to the blue sky in front of me. The weather had been full of madness all month, with sleet on Easter Day, and the Beirut–Damascus road fallen in with rain. But now the castled hill of Tibnin deployed its broken turrets through the storm, and conferred with it in a drama of forbidding beauty.

Raised on an ancient site against Tyre by the Crusading prince Hugues de Saint-Omer, lord of Tiberias, it was first called 'Toron', 'a high place'. When he died it passed to a family who took its name, and Honfroy II of Toron became constable to the king in Jerusalem, Baldwin III, and commanded respect at a time when the Crusader lords were petty and changeable. He defended Baniyas against Nureddine, and came alone to the rescue of Stephanie de Milly, besieged in Kerak while her husband was away with the king. And when Baldwin wished to negotiate a bride, it was Honfroy whom he sent to Constantinople and who returned with the emperor's thirteen-year-old niece Theodora, already handsome and well-formed.

In the spring of 1179 King Baldwin IV and the third count of Tripolis brought an army to seize flocks of sheep near Baniyas. They were suddenly attacked by a nephew of Saladin and would have been annihilated had not Honfroy, now an old man, grouped his bodyguard around him and held off the Saracens until the king was safe, and he was carried dying from the field.

From a distance his castle seemed still to honour him, solid and dependable on its rounded hill. But carved on the vaulted gateway were chained lions of the plump, Islamic sort, and inside the battlements was nothing but toppled stones. The rain flew through the loopholes and glistened on the walls. In the tower above the glacis a pair of bullocks stirred, and had rubbed off their hair against the entranceways, where it clustered like scalps.

Baibars seized the castle after Safed fell, and it was rebuilt in the seventeenth century against the Turks, and in the eighteenth by a Bedawi chief. Yet Honfroy's fortress, governed by the contours of the hill, could have differed little, and its stones have everywhere been exploited, distinctive for the bossages first used by the Phoenicians. The towers, square and semi-circular, are

[37]

made of smaller stones than the Crusaders cut, and are poorly jointed and cracking; but it is the hill itself which is the fortress of the place, steep and firm on all sides, the walls reaching sharply down its slopes, and low within. Almost alone it defied Saladin after the battle of Hattin, but was stormed in two weeks. The knights should have recaptured it ten years later under the Duke of Brabant, for they undermined the walls until the towers collapsed; but they were defeated by their own disunity and chased away.

Honfroy's son died young, and his grandson Honfroy IV was made of other stuff—a youth of beauty and learning. He was wedded to Princess Isabella of Jerusalem in the fortress of Kerak, and while the guests sang and danced, Saladin arrived and catapulted rocks against the castle. The bridegroom's mother herself cooked the marriage feast and sent out a part of it to the Saracen camp; and Saladin, asking in which tower the couple slept, was careful not to bombard it, though the younger Honfroy was renownedly effeminate and his bride was eleven years old.

Honfroy became the pawn of military men, but was too frightened or sensible to accept the crown of Jerusalem which the barons offered him in opposition to Guy of Lusignan. He was captured in 1187 at Hattin and ransomed by his mother, Stephanie of Oultrejordain, with her castles of Kerak and Montreal, but the garrisons, who did not think him worthy the exchange, refused to surrender.

A few years later his wife Isabella became heiress to the kingdom of Jerusalem, and the barons conspired to marry her to Conrad of Montferrat, who would make a formidable king. Honfroy was easily persuaded to divorce her, but she loved him and would not give him up for the gnarled Conrad and did not care to be queen. But her mother forced her to it, and Honfroy passes out of history as ambassador and confidant of Richard Coeur de Lion.

The present battlements of Toron never witnessed this. The castle was stripped in 1219 by the sultan Muadhem to prevent it ever again shielding Christians, but was rebuilt ten years later and passed to Eleonora de Montfort in dispute with the Teutonic Knights. After four centuries the Arabs raised their degenerate citadel with its stones, and seem to have exorcized its past, leaving no wraith of Honfroy in its bleak and malconstructed halls, nor of Isabella, châtelaine of a half-gratified love.

I walked south through a military checkpoint and the storm

blew round again, thick and miserable as it was when the Duke of Brabant fled absurdly back to Tyre, leaving his wounded behind him in the hail. I noticed the slit of a machine-gun post beneath the castle. A military lorry stopped and the driver smiled thinly and demanded my papers, and smiled again properly when he saw that they were in order. The division between friendliness and suspicion was vanishing. An officer followed me in a truck and demanded my papers too, and handed them back with the same apology as he might have done had he ordered me shot. The fields along the road were silent, the grey hills uncrowned. On my right birds flew with valedictory cries, and far to the left lay the dappled valley where the older Honfroy died to save his king.

After two hours I reached another post where iron road obstructions stood and some men were being searched for weapons, and a sentry let me through unwillingly. I walked between tank blocks and followed the road into the empty valleys. I had begun to feel like a fugitive from man into nature, but now nature herself was beginning to fail. It seemed as if the life of plants was bound up with that of men, as the Phoenicians thought, for the flowers were thinning away; the land was banked and hostile. The sky poured down. The miles to Israel dwindled—five, four, three—and the smooth hills of Galilee grew out of the rain.

Somewhere in front the soldiers faced one another, lost in the boredom which is the better half of war; but behind them is a hatred more obsessive than Europeans know, a tribal vendetta reborn, embers which never go to ashes. A man can hate a man harder than he can an animal, and hate his neighbour harder than another man. In Damascus and Tel Aviv even the girls are taught how to assemble a machine-gun and have learnt their enmity at school.

An old woman perched on a cliff above me grated: 'Yahoud!' Jew! and only seemed to echo the accusation of the rocks. An emptiness had been growing inside me for days; I think it began with the youth's demand that I send him fifteen pounds from England—a breach of traditional hospitality which I never met again. After that it was the face of Noha, which her parents called the will of God; and now the soldiers and the scowl of the countryside. All these seemed, in different ways, to be a denial of life, the death of the goddess, and many trivia contributed their share: the hail and the destruction of Toron and the rifled grave of Hiram. Against this only the flowers had stood, and the

[39]

faded divinities of Egypt, carved in trust and ardour long ago, when the earth was divine.

*   *   *

'Look! Israel!'
'Yes. Israel!'
'You see the fort on the hill to the left?'
'Yes.'
'England built it.'
'No.'
'In 1948, before the soldiers left. I watched it go up.'

The little tailor poured more eggs and thyme onto my plate. 'The Israelis sometimes fly over us against Syria. I have seen their planes. Then I hear boom! boom! over there.' He waved his arm eastward from the terrace of his house and over the tumbled village less than two miles from the frontier.

With us sat a schoolmaster with a face which reminded me, as Arab faces often do, of somebody I knew in the West. He showed me the white village mosque with its pile of Iraqi pebbles which the Metawilleh bring from Kerbela, where Husain, the son of Ali, was killed by Damascene soldiers. When they pray they lay these stones before them towards Mecca, and touch them with their foreheads. To the schoolmaster, everything in his village had meaning. In its walls were lodged entablatures with clear Greek dedications for a church or temple. Some ammunition-trailers and a light field-gun cluttered the main street. Nearby weak tobacco was grown, and covered with shining nylon bags to prevent the dogs from chewing it. The man was a master of calligraphy, and pointed this way and that in the streets at their multitude of signs, most of which he had written. On a single plaque he might combine the discipline of the *Naski* or *Ruq'a* with the flow of the Egyptian, or a Persian script like a scattering of swords after battle; and he inscribed shop entrances with Diwani, careful and elegant, and Kufic twined in flowers.

In the evening the hail blew down again and bounced along the village streets, and it was then that the little sallow tailor decided he would take me to a ruined city somewhere in the hills. He gave me his coat and we ran through the stepped streets, with the hail rolling after us like marbles down the gutters, and the schoolmaster cursing behind while his suit, the symbol of prestige, grew formless and clammy. We found the village taxi, climbed in with two local dignitaries, and plunged into the mud, the wind playing on the bonnet like a xylophone. We appeared to be driving into Israel, but must have been invisible, wrapped in a grey cloud such as those in which the ancient gods would bear away Homeric heroes. The taxi-driver declared that Israel was in the opposite direction; somebody else said we were probably already there, and the schoolmaster thought we were running parallel to the border. And all the time the clouds came rolling from the mountains like cannon smoke and the hail danced its mad mazurka on the rocks.

The tailor shouted 'We're here!' and we stalled at the foot of a hill. He began to climb out of the taxi, his tiny head encased in an anorak quaintly bobbled. Then he spread an umbrella and was whisked uphill by the wind, shouting and laughing, his bow legs gambolling like a satyr's from rock to rock. The taxi-driver followed slowly, saying we were all *majnun* and that there were only stones up there.

The Arabs called the city 'Shalaboun', which means 'overthrown', and I could imagine no form it might have taken, so broken was it and sunk in such a wilderness of stone. The villagers keep a tradition that their ancestors lived there, but that it was torn up by an earthquake. Fragments of red pottery dotted the ground, which changed its colour light to dark where a kiln must have been. Dry cisterns left deceitful openings in the scrub, and leaning against the slope, as if they had floated there on some diluvian flood, were a pair of stone Hellenistic sarcophagi, sculptured with cherubs holding garlands in their hands.

Sitting that night in the house of the schoolmaster, we argued about the merits of the Greeks in the Levant, disagreeing with goodwill. In his two-roomed house, thrown up from half-hewn stones, the works of Tolstoy and Dostoyevsky stared from the bookshelves, with volumes of Sartre and Simone de Beauvoir and Islamic philosophers and poets, lovingly bound. His friends were courteous and cheerful, with roving minds and socialistic views. Being poor and agricultural, they were fiercer against Israel than they felt their government to be, and christened their children Gemal Abdul Nasser.

The Moslem religion, they said, had throttled their society, and made for wretched marriages. 'Freud would enjoy himself in our village . . . but men only take one wife now; the first won't stomach a rival and makes too much row. Life wouldn't be worth living . . . and Mahomet still won't let us drink. . . .'

Two of the men held covert parties once a week, like schoolboys, downing arak and a cheap white wine in the privacy of a room. 'Education will come in the end, but we won't know that paradise. Our schooling system has scarcely changed since the French left. *Wallahi!* That's more than twenty years ago now and in France they have altered their schools four or five times. We read Chateaubriand and Lamartine. What is the use of them? They can't make a shoelace!' And as for the West: 'France gave a sick dog a pill, but it spat it out. England did the same, but it spat it out again.' A wizened history of imperialism. And as for the government . . . And as for the police, they are the potatoes of the government . . .

The night was quiet. In the room adjoining mine the schoolmaster's parents slept, like peasants from a Russian folk tale, huge and content. His father was a *hajji* who had journeyed twice to Mecca and Medinah, and had seen the grave of Husain at Kerbela and brought back in his hands a fragment of its sacred earth.

At dawn I heard an explosion far away, but nothing followed, until my door was pushed open to let in a lake of sunlight, and the tailor stood there like a leprechaun. 'Come on! The sun's here and it's a sweet day!'

5. A Smell of Orchids

For, lo, the winter is past, the rain is over and gone;

The flowers appear on the earth; the time of the singing of birds is come, and the voice of the turtle is heard in our land . . .

The Song of Solomon ii. 11, 12

NATURE GROWS MOST DESOLATE when history deserts her, like a bone without flesh; but wherever paths cross or the plough has carved a name the countryside assumes memories and is invisibly softened. The whole of Lebanon falls within this vale of recollection. There cannot be a knoll which is free from the past, and there are heights and valleys which have guided men and armies the selfsame way, as birds are ushered south in winter, one after another into oblivion.

Beaufort is such a place, built by the Romans on the corridor which linked Damascus with the sea at Tyre and Sidon, a thousand feet above the Litani river. The Arabs raised a new fortress here long after, and King Fulk of Jerusalem took it from them in 1139 and gave it to the lords of Sayette, who built it again.

From fifteen miles away the upsurge of its walls is a fable on the horizon, the round towers sharp with a metal clarity above the river. Visitors must be accompanied by two soldiers and only remain an hour, for the old fortress stands on a new frontier and from it one can see the Israeli village of Metulleh.

I was allotted a smiling, shabby soldier who put me at my ease by gleefully telling me how a Syrian corporal had fallen down the oubliette. We arrived under the ramparts. Beyond a dry, shallow reservoir the southern bastion rose, bearded in artemisia, the bossed stones of its semi-circular tower formidably smooth and intact. On one side the cliffs dropped to the constricted Litani; on the other the slopes were half grassed over, the walls savage and falling, the keep collapsed.

It is a striking compound of strength and vulnerability. The impregnable river and the high citadel are faulted by a plateau in the south offering no natural obstacle, but a level position for ballistas. The Templars tried to block it off with a new fortress, but the Mamelukes destroyed this. Now we walked by cisterns past caves which were storehouses or stables, skirted the southern towers and went in by a door unknown to the knights, whose entrance is a breach in the river wall. We ascended chambers in whose empty frames the mountains stood, blue and grey, and came to an overgrown courtyard, dangerous for attackers, who would be confronted by new walls and cut off behind by passageways. Spiralling again up stairs, a bored guide pointed out unlikely places as dungeons and bread-ovens; then the level courtyard, where the keep stood disembowelled and the western walls dipped below, quiet under the sun. In the east the tracery of a gutted hall stood up by miracle, with tierceron vaulting and ogival windows: a place of assembly perhaps, as restrained and handsome as the best Crusader work.

From this summit we looked into three countries. The ramparts dropped under us into a thousand-foot precipice down which strode grey, serrated rocks like mailed men. Along the eastern sky the crests of Hermon shone, and further north the hills sloped mildly to the Beqaa valley. The lord of Beaufort could have felt himself a god; standing on his citadel appearing strong as the mountain he could see the ships sailing to Tyre on a clear day. A beacon on the south-west wall would be noticed from Toron, a turreted shadow in the south, and to the east he could signal to Baniyas, nestled in the violence of the Syrian hills.

But life was mostly quiet and the days filled out by administrative problems. On their feudal estates the lords governed Moslem as well as Christian Arabs, who had been attracted by the efficiency and justice of their rule. At evening Arabian music was played in the courts, where the knights lounged in jewelled robes of Damascus silk and drank the wines of Syria. In Jerusalem a Frankish king held audience cross-legged in gold burnous, and Syrian eunuchs and savants mingled with Lebanese doctors.

Saladin entertained Reynald of Sidon, lord of Beaufort, for many months in Damascus and suspended his siege of the castle because he believed that the Crusader would become a Moslem; but while Reynald lingered there under truce, showing an interest in Islamic poetry and religion, Beaufort's ramparts were reinforced. In August 1189 Saladin grew tired and demanded its surrender as a pledge of good faith. Reynald was taken to the gates of the fortress, exhorted it in Arabic to surrender and in

French to stand firm, and was led back to Damascus in chains. The cisterns which sustained it are still many and deep, and its lower passages are bordered by arsenals now resonant and glistening with damp, empty as when the starved knights surrendered honourably two years later, and took Reynald back with them to Sidon.

Beaufort was restored to the Crusaders by a treaty with the sultan Ismail, but the garrison refused to evacuate and the sultan was forced to besiege his own men before the pact could be honoured. Soon after, it passed out of the dominion of Sayette and was sold to the Knights Templars. The silks and music vanished from its halls. The Templars lived in armour and began at once to build new towers in the south. Disciplined by war and religion, their order extended its control across the marches of the dying kingdom. They 'never dress gaily', wrote St Bernard, 'and wash but seldom. Shaggy by reason of their uncombed hair, they are begrimed with dust, and swarthy from the weight of their armour and the heat of the sun. . . .' They turned their swords only against the Moslems, and their backs on petty feudal interests: chaplains and serjeants of God with giant red crosses on their white surcoats, the last to give in.

In 1268, a day after part of the garrison had left for Sidon, Baibars appeared outside the walls and battered Beaufort into surrender. The women and children he sent away to Tyre, the men he took as slaves. Beaufort is seldom mentioned afterwards until Fakr ed Din refortified it against the Turks, to whom it was betrayed, and for forty days the pasha of Damascus dismantled its walls. But the castle which the Templars knew is pure beneath the ground, in the burrowed darkness of halls and dappled sunlight where lizards eavesdrop, the dream still in the rock.

*   *   *

I was rambling through the countryside at will, for the domain of the goddess is wide, and to set too definite a goal is to limit the journey, only the unobtainable being worthy of so hard a pilgrimage. The Lebanon, alone of Middle Eastern countries, draws the traveller on, now with the prospect of a mountain, now by the corridor of a river. Always there is the chance of a discovery, and along the way the deity leaves clues: plants which appear to live on nothing; hidden springs; stray carvings; and strongest of all, as I walked up the Litani, the anemones climbed with me, fresh and gay on the heights.

The deadness of the southern hills had vanished, and spray hung like incense on the river. Beneath the village of Yohmor the cliffs rose sheer six hundred feet or had broken away in drifts of grey and orange shale, where oak trees clustered and boulders hung. The river, in full spate, bellowed and thrust itself through rocks; orchards spread along its banks, shored up in deserted terraces, and here the almond blossom hung wax-like and pale, and Judas trees blushed in wide clumps against the slopes. Between the severity of the gorge and the white water the soil was filled with a scarlet audience of wind-flowers, heavy-scented broom and a dusting of many tiny plants which leant their own tint to the stones.

The last person to have written of Yohmor—a priest who came more than a hundred years ago—found a moss-covered bridge formed by fallen rocks over the river. This has been swept away, though the robbers' caves he mentioned are still there, high and tenantless in the cliffs. I found a shallow ledge, shielded in rocks and a dwarf oak tree, and I settled for the night by the clash of water cascading among stranded trees and stones. From my shelter a tiny glen descended, perhaps fifty yards long, where rocks and shrubs seemed to have been placed with the premeditation of a Japanese garden; so faithfully did nature follow art, that even to the furthest landscape trees leant quaint and angular from ridges, and many distances of mountains shed their substance, one after another, into the sky.

I expected a cold night from the tempests, feared by Phoenician sailors, which blow down the valley passages and out to sea. But the wind fell and the stars appeared so close that they tangled in the branches of the oak above my head. The nights are often no clearer than in European lands, so soon do the desert heavens lose their brilliance, but that evening one could lift a hand and graze them. I remembered other nights of watching stars, afraid that nature herself was blind and lonely. But now, framed in black rocks, they were drawn within the orbit of mankind. The North American Indians said that the stars came down and talked to them, and Esquimaux believed that they were seal-hunters who had lost their way home. All that the ancients thought, from the time of Babylon, seemed natural and likely: that stars be given names and histories and that the immortal gods should change men into light and set them in the sky. Here Pegasus spread his wings in a rosary of sparks, the Gemini sprawled their glistening limbs above the cliffs, and there stood the Little Bear, which the Greeks called 'The

Phoenician Star' after those who first sailed by it. And much later, before any sign of dawn, the Morning Star arose, worshipped by ancient Arabians as Astarte.

I awoke to the faint scent of crushed orchids. Along the river the blossom covered me with petals, and I moved through meadows so dense with cyclamen that I was forced to tread on them, as if dreaming, among heady, unidentifiable scents, to the sound of the river.

But after a mile the cliffs leant in and choked off the valley. I turned back and ascended the river bank on all fours—five hundred feet of ashen rock—feeling cast out of paradise. The only people I saw were two women working under the trees above, the only flower was the blotched and sinister dragon arum. I picked my way along the cliffs high above the sunken river until I came to an electricity generating station—a part of the Litani dam scheme—and slid over the locked gates of the bridge while its guardian was looking upriver.

On my left arose the slopes of the Mont Liban, the mountain chain which is the heart of Lebanon; to my right stood Hermon; and all afternoon these two silent companions followed me effortlessly until at dusk I saw the green lake of the newly-dammed river, followed a goat-track west into the Niha mountains and slept in a robber's cave.

The Jebel Niha is a harsh range, difficult to explore, whose rocks are strangely watered by the rain so that in the dawn they appeared like statues. Higher up I walked through snow, leaving a lonely trickle of footprints, and descended onto the road which leads to Jezzine.

Jezzine lies within the spine of mountains which is the true Lebanon, and as if to warn me that I crossed a boundary, the clouds descended onto the road, jaundiced and luminous where the sun still shone on them. In their Wagnerian twilight a partridge rose and vanished through the whiteness, and I accepted it as a portent, for the partridge was sacred to Astarte. Goats too belonged to her. So did the swan and the ram, the myrtle tree, the fish and the goose. Sparrows were offered on her altars and lions upheld her throne.

But her special emblem was the dove, too holy in Syria even to be touched, but sacrificed in flames in Cyprus. Often the Greeks portrayed the dove resting on her palm, but in the East she might hold instead the apple of generation, and the poppy, symbol of sleep and the nether world. The orange and pomegranate were also hers, emblems of fertility, and a mountain bride is still showered with orange blossom like confetti, a custom which the Crusaders brought back to Europe. Before entering her husband's home she throws an orange at him three times and grinds a pomegranate under her heel, splashing its seeds over the threshold.

The symbol of the tortoise, on whose shell the goddess placed her foot in many ancient statues, remains an enigma. Plutarch called it a reminder to women to stay in their houses and stop talking, but the sentiment is Roman and masculine, and the emblem came from the East, where it must have held some significance later forgotten. And there has survived in writing only the strange story that Thessalian women beat a rival to death with wooden tortoises in a shrine to Aphrodite.

The most complex of the animals holy to Astarte was the pig, which the Phoenicians called *alpha*, 'the cruel'. It is thought that during the cutting of corn a wild swine taking refuge in the dwindling sheaves may have been hailed as god of the harvest; whatever the reason, swine and harvest are linked, and Adonis, at some early stage, perhaps embodied both. In primitive times a boar may have been consecrated as the god and worshipped by women who believed themselves to be sows, and each year the boar was killed and torn in pieces, his death mourned and his resurrection hailed in the deification of a new boar. Early man saw little distinction between the deity and his sacrifice. A god-king was killed and replaced, and his successor killed after him. Thus if Adonis was a boar as well as a vegetation spirit, he must suffer death from a boar; and from this mystery—the offering of the god to himself—the classic legend crystallized.

In the Greek era, swine appear wherever the cult of the Great Goddess came close to that of Adonis. They were sacrificed to Aphrodite in Pamphylia and Thessaly and at the feast of pigs in Argos. At Hierapolis, a famous city of Astarte, the swine was said to be unclean and was yet too holy to be sacrificed: an ancient confusion. And in Cyprus, wrote Antiphanes, 'Aphrodite took particular pleasure in pigs.'

Alone among the holy animals, wild swine have vanished from the Lebanese mountains. Like the gods, they are officially extinct, but there are still rumours of them, and I met a farmer who swore that he had glimpsed wild pig in a thicket in the dusk.

The loneliness of the mountains is often intense. Even the villages are half-empty, the young men gone away. This massive emigration—sometimes to coastal Lebanon, often far abroad—

has left its sadness wherever the terraces are untended and the marginal fields unsown. Those who now own land are mainly of the village middle class, or city men who rent it out or hire labour. The exhausted fields, which peasant families once sowed with wheat and barley, are left bare or given over to grazing. The brushwood-gatherers—ragged even among the poor— find fuel here for the village kilns and ovens, and the goats demolish all that is green.

Even on cultivated land the plough has cut through a litter of stones, and the meanest terraces have been banked with rocks for the planting of a few olives. From beneath, the terraces ascend in giant stairways to the crags; from above they are like the whorls of fingerprints. The farmer dreams of owning trees: on the coast, banana, orange, lemon or date; higher up, apples, cherries, plums and pears. The mulberries are almost gone, for the silk market, vital a hundred years ago, collapsed with wider competition and the introduction of artificial stuffs.

Yet the farmer still speaks of his land with love. From across a valley one may hear him talking hoarsely to his oxen as if they understood long sentences, and bells jingle on their harness. Because men split up their land when they bequeath it, a farmer may own widely separate strips. He may walk miles across the glaring rocks to tend a small plot, and for an hour or two a week he guides his slender quota of water down cracked channels to the earth. His soil is ancestral and personal. His fathers gave their lives to it, and it is only sold when there is no other course. He knows each strip by name, 'The-place-of-long-rocks' or 'The-field-where-Ahmed's-oxen-ran-away' or simply 'Abu Salim', for as the psalmist wrote, 'they call their lands after their own names'. And émigrés who will never return still keep their plots and think of them, while they fall fallow. Children of the Earth Mother.

6. A Hum of Bees

Calm as thy sacred streams thy years shall flow;
Groves which thy youth has known thine age shall know;
. . . .
Still from the hedge's willow-bloom shall come
Through summer silences a slumberous hum . . .

Virgil: *Eclogues*

JEZZINE IS TYPICAL of the pretty towns and villages of the Mountain, built out of limestone and roofed with pink European tiles. Down its ravine two waterfalls glisten for a hundred and thirty feet before their rivers run together in a flower-filled valley. Its people are Maronites—Christian mountaineers—and are well known for their work in cutlery, which they decorate cheerfully with inlaid bone.

Here the mountain history begins: vestiges of families grown to power through courage and intrigue, who sometimes ruled the Lebanon independent of the Ottomans, building forts and palaces in the hills for their brief years. At Jezzine the emir Fakr ed Din took refuge in a gorge and defied the Turks with scarcely a friend beside him. Years before, his father had been trapped by the Ottomans in the redoubt of Niha-Toron not far away, and had died of poison or starvation; and the twelve-year-old prince was smuggled by his mother to a Christian family in Kesrouan, where he passed his boyhood secretly. But he grew up in his father's religion—as a Druse, the most wayward of the sects of Islam. Before he came of age he acquired command of a district, and fifteen years later became the first sole ruler of Lebanon. He was so small, it was said, that if an egg dropped from his pocket it would not break; '. . . great in courage and achievements,' wrote the traveller George Sandys, 'about the age of forty; subtill as a foxe, and not a little inclining to the Tyrant. He never commenceth battel, nor executeth any notable designe without the consent of his mother.'

Thinking three centuries ahead of his time, he envisaged a 'Greater Lebanon', free from Turkey and orientated westward. Under his rule the Roman Catholic missions first entered the Mountain, and his ports became depots for European merchants

—Florentine, Venetian and French—where Lebanese silks, olive oil and cereals were exported with profit. So Fakr ed Din was able to pay an army of forty thousand mercenaries and refortify the decayed march castles of the Crusaders. He bought European artillery, furnished patrols for his roads, and financed spies and his own faction in the court at Constantinople.

In 1618 he was forced to flee to Italy, where for five years he was fêted by the nobility. But he returned to the Mountain and governed it again, transferring his winter residence from Sidon to Beirut, where he built a palace with many stables and dens of lions, and decorated it with statues on pedestals from which, said Maundrell, 'it may be infer'd, that this *Emir* was no very zealous Mahometan'. Perhaps it is true that Fakr ed Din was secretly a Christian, but toward the Ottomans he behaved as a Moslem, and as a Druse when he returned to the hills, until his power extended from Aleppo to Jerusalem and he was called 'Sultan of the Land'.

When his star fell he took refuge in the fortified galleries of Niha-Toron, where his father had died thirty-six years before; but the source of his water-supply was betrayed to the Turks, who poisoned it by slaughtering animals there. So one night he fled to Jezzine and was guided to a cave along a path against the mountain. Here the Turks, by mining beneath the grotto and smoking out its defenders, at last captured Fakr ed Din. Two years later, as a prisoner in Constantinople, he was strangled by mutes, and it was said that a Christian cross was found among his clothes.

The farmers of Jezzine told me that the grotto was inaccessible now, and infested by snakes. But I found it in the cliffs above a tangled hill, far from their orchards. The rock-cut path which the emir took, though crumbling and so low that one must often crawl, still reaches the entrance. It is scarcely more than three feet square, and overgrown, like a natural cave; but inside I saw that grooves had been cut in the passageway, where four successive doors had sealed it.

A black snake melted into darkness like a spirit. From the gallery a shaft led upwards and cobwebs hung from the soft limestone ceilings like acrobats' netting; there may have been a snail staircase once, but the Turks had burnt everything, and I wedged my feet among the crevices to climb into the upper gallery. The rampart closing its entrance had broken down, so that the sun shone on a floor bright with watercress and in its jagged breach the mountains stood, tragically beautiful.

The Castle of Abu l'Hassan

The Palace at Beit-ed-din

Gorges of the Litani

Into the rock-face behind had been cut a corridor where my torch-beam awoke long, glistening streams. It was as if the emir had hoped to hew his way to the other side of the mountain, but after a hundred yards I reached the end, where the walls had been idly gashed, then suddenly abandoned.

I took a road from Jezzine which soon became a track, past hills of umbrella pines, smooth as mushrooms. The Jezzine and Barouk rivers met in an oasis of light. Here and there were farmhouses of handsome stone, broken in among cistus, victims of the 1956 earthquake which shook the valley of habitation. And near the water's confluence stood an Arab bridge, whose lower stones might have been Roman cut; and four granite columns were sunk to their necks in the ground.

This was the ancient city of Borri, now an orchard of bitter oranges, falling ungathered. Borri is scarcely mentioned by ancient chroniclers, but gave its name to the Bostrenus river, which forms there. It must always have occupied a position of beauty and usefulness, for through it the route from Sidon bent north to Damascus into a valley secretive with hills; and another may have linked it to the road passing out of Tyre over Hermon, or joined the highway paved by Trajan from the Red Sea. On either side the rivers flow down into its stillness, and a Roman road reaches it through pine-woods in the north-west.

The granite columns, very large for so small a town, could only have been raised for a god, and the Jezzine river nearby has rubbed away its banks and uncovered the base of the temple. It appears to have been heavily made: the tribute of a merchant city with money in lieu of taste. Probably it was dedicated to Eshmun, whom the Romans linked with Aesculapius, for the river on which it stood, 'the graceful Bostrenus', was itself held sacred to him and finds the sea near his temple at Sidon.

I started along its valley by the last of the Wadi Barouk, and noticing Roman stones beneath my feet, looked down into the river. There under the green water shone the streets and pavements of the ancient city, level and straight as they were first laid. In that miasmal light the fragments moved and glittered, as if the city quickened into life; from its smoothed foundations the roofs and porticoes grew through water toward the sky, scraping the river's surface: a whole city. Here the farmers planted vines and olives, and merchants came, bringing perfumes and Cappadocian horses, cassia and the Adonis cult. And the river, which has rediscovered this, is easing out its stones and rolling them, one by one, toward the sea.

*   *   *

The earthquake valley is at peace now, emptied of men, the harsh strata of its hills wooded in many nuances of green. The river is broad and shallow, flowing through an almost English meadow, in which I met a lone farmer who seemed to be the guardian of its silence. I saw a dove. Beyond, land which had once been ploughed was shingle and maquis now, and the river banks were ruptured with trees torn up and thrown into the water. Up the southern hills I followed the road first built through pine-woods by the Romans, who cut grooves in the rock for drainage and laid paving-stones, now almost gone. In the dusk I arrived at the door of the Machmouche monastery.

This is a Maronite foundation, and patron of the surrounding lands, housing two hundred students of all religions. Built like a fortress where a pagan temple may have stood, its windows look down to convents on many knolls, and glimpse beyond—drawn in a low curtain under the sky—the Mediterranean. The Father Superior gave me a room for the night. I remember him only as taciturn, with a blue shirt peeping over his penitential black robes. But in the monastery I found a Frenchman, who had been sent to teach his language under the military service scheme for pacifists.

'I nearly died of cold this winter. The wind blew straight through the walls. At night I wore two pairs of pyjamas, trousers, shirts, dressing-gowns, socks, anything I could find, and put my face under the pillow. And I asked to be posted to Lebanon because of the heat here.'

We drank Benedictine in his room. He was mentally scratching out each day, each hour, before he could return to Lille to join his father's textile factory and marry the girl whose pretty face comforted him from photographs around the bare walls. 'The people here are kind, but like children. One grows idiotic. Sometimes I can't stand it. . . .' A bell sounded. 'We must eat dinner with the fathers now; they are certain to offer us their local wine in your honour. You cannot avoid drinking it, because they watch you. So just swallow and do not think of *anything.* . . .'

In the morning a monk showed me the building. Its passages

sucked up the two hundred students like dust, but it was more like a school than a monastery: lockers and gloom. From behind many doors came the tapping of billiard cues, the wail of chalk over blackboards and voices of irritated authority: 'Now will you repeat after me . . .'

The history of the monastery is like many in the south—barely two and a half centuries old, but filled with troubles. The Maronites are the dominant sect in Lebanon—a mountain people and a prosperous bourgeoisie, dark-haired and stocky. Their origins are confused, but their religion gained prominence thirteen hundred years ago, when the Byzantine emperor Heraclius stayed at the monastery of St Maron on the Orontes. He was searching for a compromise to unite the two main factions in his empire: the Monophysites, strong in Egypt and Syria, who believed in the single nature of Christ, and the orthodox, who saw Him compounded of two elements, God and man.

Heraclius found that the monks of St Maron believed in a dual Christ, but that His will was single. Hoping to reconcile his realm, the emperor proclaimed this as the orthodox view, and so created a new sect, which was declared a heresy in 680. A few years later Justinian II sacked the monastery of St Maron, but its schismatics had already spread into north Lebanon. Here their influence grew. The Abbasids persecuted them, but in the mountains they were victorious. They supplied the Crusaders with guides and archers, and some even left for Cyprus when the Holy War was lost. At about this time their church recognized the leadership of Rome, but kept its liturgy in Syriac, an adaptation of the Roman Mass, as it does still, with its own saints and many minor customs.

The Deir Machmouche is modern, except for a part of the cloister and for its chapel, whose walls were cracked by earthquake. The Druses had galloped in during the 1860 battles and had killed eighteen monks and burnt it, so that afterwards the doorway was built too low for a horseman to enter, and an alcove had been left black with the fire, as a warning or as a memorial. The cloisters have been rebuilt white and simple on an upper story. 'Austerity is proper,' said my guide, and the monks' faces in their twilit cells were those of Merlin and the Venerable Bede.

*   *   *

In the Books of Kings it is recorded that the Israelites 'set them up images and groves in every high hill, and under every green tree: And there they burnt incense in all the high places, as did the heathen. . . .' Solomon turned away from God and built a high place to Astarte, and Josiah 'brake in pieces the images and cut down the groves, and filled their places with the bones of men'. But the holiness of these sanctuaries was of the hills themselves, and so natural was their veneration to Semitic peoples that no king or prophet could destroy them, and often the Jews took and resanctified them.

'Joshua came with an army and captured high places all over this district,' said a monk of Deir Machmouche, pointing into the mountains, and gave Jewish names to the peaks around: Nebi Hanania, Nebi Azar, Nebi Ayyoub. On the hill behind us were the tombs of a Hebrew prophet named Nebi Misha and his wife, but nobody knew who they were or what they had done. Beside them, in a circle of stones, grew a sacred oak tree, so old that its trunk had died, and new branches sprang from its base. The small, domed tombs were venerated by local Moslems, who had covered one with silks in Islamic green and lit iron lamps where candle-wax bled to the floor.

These sanctuaries must have fallen and been rebuilt era beyond era. The lamps which were lit in the shrines of Astarte are rededicated, but only to another name. On the tomb walls of the prophetess—if such she was—sacred trees have been lightly moulded. Here Moslems ask things of the saint which they would be shy to ask of God, and women petition the unknown lady for fertility.

Shrines like these grow from half the crags and knolls of Lebanon, rude-walled and white-domed under trees descendent from the pagan groves. Every village has its saint's tomb, or *weli*. Sometimes they belong to mad or holy men who actually lived, but more often the villagers know nothing of their origin. 'A great prophet is buried there', they say, or 'a famous lady who died long ago'; or sometimes, embarrassed by the absence of any grave, they declare that a holy man or woman passed that way and so the place is blessed.

If the site is ancient, the name of its saint is usually that of a misty patriarch perpetuated through all the Semitic religions, and perhaps born in Phoenician myth. So the names in the high places alter or are lost, but the sanctity never fades. Significantly, many of the shrines are those of women, and often a woman is associated with the *weli* of a man. 'She was his sister', they say, or 'she was his daughter'. Rarely is she a wife, for the moral sense of Moslems and Christians turned the divine Phoenician lovers into consanguinity.

As if the Great Goddess still opened her arms impartially to all life, the shrines are sought out by every sect. Christians, Metawilleh and Druses, who shun each other's mosques or churches, murmur prayers together before the unknown spirits on the hilltops, and tie strips of sick relatives' clothing to the bars of the windows or on the holy tree as a talisman for health, and sometimes give a small gift, or offer henna as libation.

Mythologists say that in Lebanon Adonis became St George, who is called enigmatically 'El Kudr', 'The Green One'. Wherever the Adonis cult was popular in ancient times, the sanctuaries to The Green One abound, and petitioners to his chapels, moulding his character to their needs, still ask for health and fertility, and so preserve his early nature.

So Adonis and Astarte have left their footprint in the nemoral *welis*. And since it was always the privilege of oriental deities to hide behind many names, The Green One and the Unknown Lady may be accepted as clues along the way.

*   *   *

I reached the Monastery of Our Lady at that late hour of afternoon when the sun sheds a gold, intimate patina, and softly stretches shadows. The monastery stood high and alone where the Bostrenus gorge narrowed and the mountain spurs grew steep. Near the chapel walls I listened to a sound like cymbals (which was the grating of the priest's censer) and thought I had stumbled on a pagan rite. Through the garden spread lines of weathered hives, and the purr of bees drowned the whole monastery, consuming the chanting of the monks, so that often one could not tell which was which, nor free the smell of incense from the scent of clover.

When the prayers ended, novices filed back into the seminary and the Superior, stepping through the door as if from an ikon, raised his arms slowly in welcome. The monastery, he said, had not always been so quiet. Twice the pasha of Acre had burnt and pillaged it, Egyptian soldiers looted its treasures, and in 1860 the Druses killed ten priests, who lay buried in a cave below. But since, there had been a century of silence. He showed me round the building and there was little to see: wooden beds, bells and a flour-mill; doves and rabbits. His days were spent in training priests and keeping bees. The hives with painted figures belonged to farmers, but those inscribed with crosses—and these were most numerous—housed monastic bees. Quietness, he said, was an avenue to God.

That night I reached the Deir Moukalles, Monastery of the Holy Saviour. It is more complex and important than the Monastery of Our Lady, whose duty is to train some of its novices and to supply it with honey. In the smaller foundation I had been unaware that the priests belonged to any sect, but I realized now that I was in a stronghold of the Greek Catholics, who professed the orthodoxy of the Byzantine emperor after the Council of Chalcedon and were rudely dubbed 'Melkites' or 'king's men'. They recognize the authority of the Pope, but for their liturgy they use the Byzantine rite and their churches, vestments and beliefs are close to those of the Greek Orthodox.

I was greeted at the gate by a very old priest, whose forehead was creased into a permanent ridge by his *kalimaikon* and whose beard smelt of peppermint. The Greek Catholic priests seem to grow more energetic as they age. Father Gregoire attacked steep stairways with wheezing purpose, bowled along cloisters and showed me the whole monastery, speaking in a rich and gusty voice which passed through many tones in a single sentence.

'The monastery was founded by a miracle. It was in 1711 when the bishop of Tyre and Sidon—Euthyme Saifi—was passing in procession to Damascus. Somebody had a new gun and one of the deacons, who must have been interested in firearms, wished to hold it, and shot a priest in the stomach. The deacon was Athanasi Nasr, but I do believe I have forgotten the name of the priest—a follower of Saifi. Was it Father . . .? Yes it was! It was Father Ibrahim Toutou!' His face fractured into wrinkles of rejoicing. 'It was Father Toutou! Shot in the tummy!'

'What then?'

'The bishop cried out "Holy Saviour!" '

'Yes?'

'And Toutou got up and blessed himself and was alive!'

'The bullet had bounced off his tummy-button.'

'No! No! The priest had a metal disc under his soutane.'

'That was cheating.'

'A miracle! Certainly a miracle! You see, the gun fired pellets, not bullets—a shotgun—and the pellets melted on his stomach and formed the disc! So the bishop declared that a monastery be built on the spot and called the Monastery of the Holy Saviour. And here we are.'

He fixed me with one laughing eye while the other, which was of glass, remained austere. The moon had stepped over the ruined cloister and still his tour continued. 'The earthquake did damage here, but we have renovated most of it. Think! We began with only seven monks.'

The Deir Moukalles is huge now and serves the whole countryside. It owns a college and an orphanage, the seminary and a convent of Holy Sisters on the hill nearby, and its priests are missionaries abroad.

When Father Gregoire had at last finished, he passed me on to a nun. She had a face wide open to the world, her features only incidents upon a pool of calm. She looked like the White Queen from *Through the Looking Glass*, and bowed to me in a starched flurry, her voice lilting, 'Welcome, specially, welcome! Here is your room, and if there is anything you want you need only ask *me*. Here is a basin and here is the W.C. There is the refectory, and an ikon of Our Lady to guard you.'

I stayed a week in Deir Moukalles. Every morning the White Queen tapped on my door and reminded me of breakfast. I ate in the guests' hall, usually alone, but sometimes the monks would take their meals with visiting relations. I grew used to raw broad beans and to watching the monks eat. They assembled their dishes of food around them like generals marshalling regiments, and were always shouting for reinforcements. Noodles and egg-pies, *markouk* and the *lebne* yoghourt vanished into their beards, and canteens of soup were absorbed with a noise like draining bath-water. This destruction occupied no time at all, but when the little coffee-cups arrived the monks grew dilatory, sniffing and sipping, and leant back in their chairs becalmed.

The peace of Deir Moukalles was intermittently broken— nuns singing down the passages, or the kitchen servants smashing something—but it was peace all the same. The Deir partook of that blended strength and meekness which is special to some monasteries, assuring for the white stillness of its rooms, its iron doors and stone-flagged passages, vaulted burrows where monks moved without talking; walls strong and quiet as faith.

Its stairs were banked with exotic plants in painted pots. There was a printing press, a library and a musky manuscript room which Father Gregoire said contained two incunabula and a history of St Francis of Assisi, written by one of his disciples soon after his death. And in the courtyard lay the marble capitals of Byzantine columns, delicate and luminous, brought from Sidon to be built into the monastery.

The chapel dated from the Deir's foundation and was sober and spacious but poorly constructed. Eleven years before, the earthquake had shaken the plaster from its walls in cloudy heaps, and it still lay there. The woodwork screens were covered with celluloid bags and the ikons had been locked away behind a morbid stucco-inlaid ikonostasis of Italian craftsmanship in an oriental style. Only the pulpit stood uncovered, a marble tulip on its slender stem; and a chandelier, given by Louis XV, glistened in the gloom like an aerial waterfall.

Mass was now celebrated in another room. The Melkites are proud that their rite is close to that of Byzantium, the liturgy of St Basil which St John Chrysostom revised. They differ from the Orthodox only in a custom of the deacon, who bows his forehead to the altar during the *cherubikon*—the hymn to which the imperial procession once moved through the royal doors of Haghia Sophia.

Father Gregoire's Mass was the most simple. He felt that the surroundings were wrong. The room was plain and small, lined with portraits of bishops and archimandrites bearded like gods, and a photograph of the President of Lebanon. The service proceeded in a nasal Arabic, except for the disembodied 'Kyrie Eleison' issuing from a sleepy monk near the *prothesis*. Shorn of its doorways and pillared distances, the great rite palled, like a pageant in plain clothes. The priests mumbled cabbalistically and the congregation was silent.

'Our people do not always worship well,' said the father. 'They are rather like Italians, always asking God to give them things: a better house or a baby. It is profane.' And like Italians they usually approach an intermediary, the Virgin or a saint. God Himself is daunting and remote, spread like a feat of science in a dome. But the saints are close and real. They may be kissed, fondled and wept over, as the Holy Mother may, though portrayed not as a spaniel-eyed Madonna but on abstract, intellectual ikons. And most Byzantines, I thought, must have worshipped like this too: the withdrawn divinity of the Panto-crator complemented by the tutelary saint, like a Roman house-god.

This is the language of faith and emotion, grown from the country of Astarte. Here it is natural to believe, and the priest is the expression of the layman. Men see God large and unalterable on every horizon and accept Him without inquiry. And partly because belief demands no spiritual strife, no step into the dark, the priest seems often to be scarcely religious at all— but a rough, believing layman in a cassock, discomfortingly practical, who goes through his devotions like a drab wizard recounting spells.

'How do I know anything?' demanded Father Gregoire. 'I do not. How does this coffee go down my throat?' he cried, spilling it into his beard. 'I do not know. How does my heart beat? My eyes see? Who made this life? To say there is no Creator is absurd.' His face was uplifted, crossed with a radiant smile. 'Think of one simple thing. Think of a glance. A man sees a woman—I excuse myself for I am a priest—but think of that glance; it may be the catalyst of new life! From this point God may ordain children! Is not that a miracle?'

This too was the voice of the East, untraceably old. When its tyranny was first challenged I do not know, but it was the Greeks who first broke through the surface of faith into the air of reason. The first civilizations, though they accumulated knowledge, explained it in terms of myth and magic. But early in the sixth century before Christ, in the Ionian state of Miletus, Thales asked himself 'What is the world made of?' and answered 'Water.' And so he became the first known scientist. It was his question, not his answer, which was significant, for he was trying to explain what lay around him, and found water where all other men had seen God. Thereafter, little by little, faith had to defend itself against reason, and was dignified or shamed by it.

Father Gregoire knew this. He had studied in Rome for eleven years, seen many museums and enjoyed the classical myths, with a guilty penchant for the battle of the Gods and Titans.

'Still people often do not think,' he said. 'There is a serving-maid who came here about fifty years ago and worked in the kitchens, asking only for food and a dress. She never misses a Mass. Every day she sits in the chapel—three or four hours— kneeling and praying. What can she have to say? She knows nothing. I have often wondered what that woman says to God all those hours. . . .' His face fell to a wrapt misery. 'Now our young people don't believe so much. Alas, they even say there is no God.'

I had noticed this too. Young Arabs, practical, and quick with solutions, are beginning to say that God is a fraud.

'But what of our brains?' cried the father. 'We may buy or sell with them, but we cannot use them to judge the universe!' Science might apply to one sphere, but could not penetrate all, for it was a product of men's minds, bound for ever to the human delusion; 'he hath set the world in their heart, so that no man can find out the work that God maketh from the beginning to the end'.

The father looked on this mystery with respect and joy, as a man sees a fine tree, knowing that it is older than him, and will live on after he is dead.

'One must preserve humility.'

But surely, I asked, belief could not be based on anything so passive as humility?

'Of course not. Faith is a gift.'

Did God, then, make men's instincts truer than their minds?

The father did not know. A man was as God made him. The father would not place the eternal within the judgement of man.

So we talked across the river of faith; hands which touch, but do not hold.

*   *   *

On my last day the White Queen served me local wine at breakfast and I felt unsteady. Father Gregoire was smelling flowers outside the monastery walls, plucking marguerites.

'When we were children,' he said, 'we used to consult the marguerite. Children do that in Italy still.' He picked a petal from the white flower. 'You go.' Then another—'You don't go'— and splintered off the petals, laughing. 'You go. You don't go. You go. You don't go. *You don't go.*' The last blade fell into the grass and he looked up with a shy smile. 'Silly.'

Almost within sight of Deir Moukalles, near the village of Joun, Lady Hester Stanhope spent her last twenty years living in a monastery which she had bought from a Damascene merchant. It was once imposing, set among olives within sight of the sea, and she had shaded it with a garden of trees and roses; but since the earthquake cracked its wall, nobody had lived there. The past April, the most rainy in memory, had left the flowers knee-high, and under its olive trees like old men's sinews, the marigolds beamed in massed, joyful banks, gashed with anemones. The groves were filled with birds singing, but these were the only sounds, and the wind bending the grass on the hill.

Lady Hester came to the East after the death of her uncle, William Pitt, and of Sir John Moore, who died at Corunna breathing her name. She had acted as Pitt's social hostess in Downing Street, and after his death her life was dull in England. By the flamboyance and daring of her entry into Damascus and her ride through the desert to Palmyra, she acquired a mystique among the Arabs. At first she settled in the convent of Mars Elias near Sidon, using her money and influence to support the Ottoman government and the interests of the French. After a French colonel was murdered in the Nosairi mountains, she took soldiers from the pasha of Acre and led a recriminatory raid which sacked over fifty villages and killed a hundred men. During civil riots her house at Mars Elias was filled by refugees, and finding the convent too small, she moved to Joun.

Little by little she became engrossed in magic and astrology; but her spies still came and went by secret entrances in new disguises, and Bedawi sheikhs pleaded audience at her gates. During the Moslem riots after Navarino the whole Christian population of Sidon camped beneath her walls, and when Mahomet Ali seized Syria, she formed herself a bodyguard of fugitive Albanian soldiers, and caused him more discomfort than any other power in the mountains.

But her imperiousness was blurring into eccentricity. She slapped and beat her servants with a mace, and the rooms at Joun were fantastic with rubbish. Down the twilit corridors tiptoed black slaves, and in the halls stirred herbalists and astrologers and a lunatic soothsayer, an ex-general of Napoleon. Her stables were occupied by a white mare and its deformed foal, 'the horse born saddled', on which she and the Messiah would ride to Jerusalem at the second coming.

A little maid had come with her from England. Withered to a fallen leaf, she was kept a half-prisoner in Joun, where she died of a black dose and was buried under the sycamore trees at Deir Moukalles.

Lady Hester became ill and recluse. She shaved her head, dressed like an Ottoman effendi in cashmeres and silk, and because her beauty was paling, entertained her guests at dusk, talking with them through the night. She had a tête-à-tête with the Duc de Richelieu, discussed the occult with a Polish nobleman, and astrology with a German princeling. The Count Laborde, who visited her in 1827, thought her mad and was convulsed by laughter. Lamartine, five years later, respected and romanticized her. 'Lady Hester appears to be about fifty years old', he wrote (she was fifty-six). 'She has those features which years cannot alter. The freshness, colour, and grace of youth, are gone; but when the beauty is in the figure itself, in the chasteness of the outlines, in the dignity, majesty, and expression of a male or female face, it changes at the different epochs of life, but it does not pass away.'

She permitted him to walk through her garden 'where I allow nothing profane to enter', and to view her horses, because his stars were favourable. 'I found that no chord was wanting in her high and strong intellect, and that every key that was touched gave out a just, full, and powerful sound, except perhaps the metaphysical chord, which too much stretching and solitude had rendered false.'

But Lady Hester thought Lamartine rather unwholesome 'with his straight body and straight fingers and self-conscious airs and graces'.

Kinglake, less illusioned, visited her three years after, and called her 'a good, businesslike, practical prophetess', who, when not talking astrology, became 'the sort of woman that you some-times see, I am told, in London drawing-rooms—cool, decisive in manner, unsparing of enemies, full of audacious fun, and saying the downright things that the sheepy society around her is afraid to utter'.

But now she was consumptive, her figure gaunt and shrunken, her teeth rotted. She could scarcely walk from the house, though at night she would sometimes grope to her garden. She coughed up blood. Most of her servants left her, taking everything valuable with them, and the monastery decayed, for she was deep in debt, and she blocked up all but one of its entrances.

In the summer of 1839 the British consul in Beirut, hearing that she was ill, rode out to Joun with an American missionary. They arrived at night, and finding the place deserted, passed down the corridors until they saw Lady Hester dead, with everything around her stolen except the ornaments on her body.

At midnight they carried her into the garden, and buried her in the vault according to her wishes, by the side of a captain in Napoleon's Imperial Guard, whom she had loved and who had died of overeating and gastritis.

'When at length I entered the arbour,' wrote the missionary, whose account is over-imaginative, 'the first thing I saw were the bones of the general [sic], in a ghastly heap, with the head on top, having a lighted taper stuck in either eye-socket. . . . It was difficult to proceed with the service. . . .

'The morning after the funeral the consul and I went round the premises and examined *thirty-five* rooms, which had been sealed up by the vice-consul of Sidon to prevent robbery. They were full of trash. One had forty or fifty oil jars of French manufactures, old, empty, and dusty. Another was crammed with Arab saddles, moth-eaten, tattered, and torn. They had belonged to her mounted guard.'

Lady Hester's pampered horses were bought by a Beirut merchant and died of overwork. Many rooms were pulled down and the stones sold to the villagers of Joun; and when the missionary returned nearly twenty years later, he found the tomb already decaying. 'There is no inscription—not a word in any language. . . .'

Some time later the place was bought by Deir Moukalles, whose monks petitioned the British embassy for a proper sepulchre for Lady Hester, but were refused. Now all that remains is the husk of the west façade and some roofless rooms, grouped round a courtyard where the Albanian guards had lingered.

The Joun villagers still talk of her as the 'Sitt' or 'Lady', and have a 'Café Lady Hester Stanhob'; but now that the Deir es Sitt is empty, it knows no intrusive element, only a pile of sunflowers on a weft of clover, and a few mulberry trees which sprawl in maudlin death among the stones. The tomb lies a hundred yards from the house on a terrace of olives: three limestone tiers and a casket, on which is inscribed 'Lady Hester Lucy Stanhope, Born 12th March 1776, Died 23rd June 1839'.

The place is so steeped in her eccentric and vital person that this desolation seems cruel in its simplicity: like a judgement. But life had treated her with a subtle harshness. At the centre of politics and society in England she had reached her zenith, but this, like scaling a mountain summit, could only bring a moment's exhilaration; for what is possessed is rarely valued. After, perhaps, there came the vision of insignificance, which causes success to kill itself, a suspicion that in the Holy of Holies there was nothing. For Lady Hester, in her sane and practical days, must have known that the stars would not answer her.

*   *   *

I climbed down the gorges of the Awali river. On the ridge above stood the convent of Holy Sisters, a child of Deir Moukalles, and not far away I imagined the Monastery of Our Lady, drowned in bees. I walked through pines like a schoolboy passing among prefects. For all the river's passion, the scene was as still as a lithograph, choked to silence by the height on which I stood. The deep wound of the valley passed through shadow out of sight, where the river turned slowly almost upon itself and a castled headland rose.

I descended rocks five hundred feet, and trusting that none of the holy sisters was promenading on the mountainside, took off my clothes and waded with them across the river. The valley was resonant and austere with the water's raging. In all the landscape there was not a terrace on which a house might rest, no sign even of a goat; only a labyrinth of treeless walls and the sunlight faintly flowing through the porches of the mountains. But as I rounded the crag I saw the castle dissembled there, savage and improbable, clasping its gates and walls against the rock.

It is a castle without history, perhaps raised by the Crusaders to link Niha-Toron with Sidon, but rebuilt by Arabs who named it Qalat Abu l'Hassan. Caged by the mountain and the loop of the river, it did not seem to be the product of men's hands at all, but the canvas of a Böcklin or a Piranesi. On its summit the battlements were soft with grass and clover, and the rooms which had been built there were ruined. At dusk bats detached themselves from the ceilings of the tower in which I slept, and owls mocked each other from the valley. The moon rose and stood in the slit window, and seemed to open up the scents of flowering thyme, leaving a snake of light upon the river.

Some people have thought the moon to be male, which is surely mistaken. She is gentle and changeable, the archaic symbol of the Great Mother, and Lucian, who was himself a Syrian, called Astarte 'the moon goddess'. Love and lunacy, dreams without interpretation, are hers by right, and lying half awake I saw a wyvern creep into the river, and heard the gremlins snoring in the trees. The senses are the only witness for the mind; so one cannot know anything, and against this fact all others blunt themselves. Who, after all, was Thales, to say that the world was made of water? The miracle was consciousness itself: that I was here now, with these stones beneath my fingers, brought to awareness between two voids.

7. The Mountain Kings

> A fountain of gardens, a well of
> living waters, and streams from
> Lebanon.
>
> *The Song of Solomon iv. 15*

NORTH FROM DEIR MOUKALLES the monasteries vanish
from the hilltops. At Gharifeh I saw women with the diaphanous
Druse headscarf called *mandil,* and when I reached the town of
Baaklin the Druse sheikhs appeared, theatrical in their *aba*s and
white-turbaned fezes. The long visages of the desert, receding
from heavy noses, had disappeared. The Druse faces were broad
and short, often pale-skinned, handsome, with stubborn chins.
Stocky like the Christian mountaineers, they have a glint of
yellow hair which is unknown among the Maronites. The
children stare up through startling grey eyes and a few of the
women, who are beautiful, are fair as harvest.

The Druses came from south Arabia, wandering north at some
unknown times, accumulating Persian paleness. The anthropologist Von Luschan, who studied a group minutely, said that
no single man fell within the range of the real Arab. Not only
must they have become changed through intermarriage, but
they were probably joined by other, purely Persian tribes, with
Mesopotamian peoples.

Benjamin of Tudela in 1170 found them living beneath the
slopes of Mount Hermon. 'They are called heathens and
unbelievers, because they confess to no religion. Their dwellings
are on the summits of the mountains and in the ridges of the
rocks, and they are subject to no king or prince. . . . This people
live incestuously; a father cohabits with his own daughter, and
once every year all men and women assemble to celebrate a
festival, upon which occasion, after eating and drinking, they
hold promiscuous intercourse. . . .'

Tales of orgies and phallic worship surrounded them, for they
keep their religion secret, and the same rumours still haunt the
lonely Nosairis, who worship in sacred groves on the mountains
of west Syria. But the Druse religion agrees with the Druse
origins and is linked to the mediaeval Persian sects, the Batenites,

who partook of the high moral teaching of Zoroaster. Drusism became the temple of many cults, fossilized and half understood: the contending light and darkness of Magianism, and the transmigration of souls; Gnosticism; Islam; Neo-Platonism; and a thread of Christianity in which a Druse Christ took the body of the Christian One from the tomb.

God, they claim, is One, the heart of life. He has been incarnate many times, but lastly as the tenth-century caliph Hakim of Egypt. Hakim has been called 'the Caligula of the East', and like Caligula he wished to become a god. He sacked the Christian shrines throughout his empire, killed all the dogs in Cairo because one barked at him, and organized a three-day massacre and conflagration there, mounting the heights above the city to watch.

After his murder, several of his followers fled to Lebanon, and found in the mountains a Persianized sect of the Shia, to whom they taught the divinity of Hakim. To increase the number of the faithful, they permitted promiscuity, and it is probably this, now abandoned, which gave the Druses their dark reputation. Burckhardt, who travelled much among them, said that they were allowed to marry their sisters, an echo from the custom of Persian kings. Hakim, they say, will return in 1996, a thousand years after his death, to judge the world, when the spirits of Light and Time will ride before him on brightly-coloured horses out of China. The Moslems will be transformed to dogs with painted coats, and the Christians be carriers of fuel and water, doomed to wear black discs in their ears, which will scorch or freeze them with the changing seasons.

The Druses ignore, more or less, the eccentric elements in their books and concentrate on 'lifting up their hearts to God' and on a code of love and truthfulness. Especially they are invoked to help each other, and this, in the days when their feudal system was rigid, gave them the cohesion of a military order. Their strangeness lies in the difference between their manner—they are famous for their courage and robustness, and always look a person in the eye—and the complexity and dissimulation in their religion. For when they find it useful they will pretend to adopt Christianity or Islam, and say, in contradiction to their beliefs, that there are many paths to God.

Every Thursday the initiates of a village assemble at its *kalweh*, a house of council on a nearby hill. I visited two of them at Baaklin: simple rooms in subdued light, with divans spread around their walls and the tomb of a holy man in the centre of

In the Jezzine valley

The Phrygian sound

Father Gregoire

each. One in seven of the Druses, male or female, is chosen as an initiate *'uqqal*, a 'Knowledgeable One', and must exceed the age of forty. Baaklin had many of them, and since the town is famous for the longevity of its inhabitants, the Knowledgeable Ones were mostly hugely-bearded and decrepit, like fairy-tale kings. The distinctive fez and long black *aba*, once the simplest vestments in the Mountain—for the *'uqqal* was forbidden to dress gaudily—are now the most flamboyant. But their wearers train themselves in stateliness and reserve. They answer questions circumspectly, or merely gesture with princely condescension. Any form of strife goes against their religious convictions. They neither smoke nor drink. Some refuse to see a doctor in their illness and this, at least in Baaklin, has preserved them into senility. There were frosty, pale-eyed *'uqqal*, who leant on sticks and moved like blind men; women *'uqqal* with pleated hair; and olympian figures whose beards hung crisp and coarse below their waists in solid mats. Confabulating in the *kalweh*, tucking their legs beneath them on the divans, there was little to be seen but turbans and beards. A stranger is sometimes allowed into these councils but learns nothing, for the Bible or Koran is respectfully read to him, according to his religion, and only after he has gone are the sacred books brought out. Afterwards the lesser *'uqqal* retire, while the senior *ajawid*, 'the Righteous', who wear striped *aba*s, confer on local affairs with coffee and solemnity.

The rest of the Druses, the 'Ignorant Ones', are apprised of only a part of the holy creed. It was an Ignorant One who invited me to stay at his home—a retired soldier who tended an orchard and lived content with a fair-skinned wife on the edge of Baaklin. Their home was typical of the Mountain, its rooms tall and bare with floors tiled for summer coolness, vases of plastic flowers on low tables, and chickens patrolling the passages.

Twenty-five years of campaigning had left the man spare and harrowed, but with large, harmless eyes behind spectacles held together with green string. He was a very happy Ignorant. An *'uqqal*'s life was too austere. He enjoyed a pipe occasionally, and when managing a French army canteen he had grown fond of Vermouth and bad language. As a child during the Great War, his parents had taken him to the Druse Mountain in southern Syria because there was famine in Lebanon, and during the mandate, in 1925, the French had attacked the rebellious people there.

'Nine hundred of them with cannon! Under General Michaud I think it was. A most rotten general anyway. Only fourteen or

fifteen of them got away!' His grin was like a crack across a nut.
'And we beat them properly, not from a distance. First we fired
our rifles. Puck! Puck! Then we rushed on them with swords.
Shre! Shre! Shre!' His arms flailed about him and phantom heads
rolled along the carpet like billiard-balls. 'Everything was
ribbons!'

I asked if he had killed a man.

'You never know in war. It's all chaos.'

'But surely, with a sabre?'

He looked a little abashed. Actually, he said, during the battle
he was in Beirut. But he had heard all about it. He had *almost*
been there. Some time later the French had enlisted him and he
had earned two pounds a month.

'But I managed the canteen. Everything was cheaper then.
Bully-beef, one franc! Small bottle of Dubonnet, two francs!
Tunny-fish, demi-franc! But then I had to fight again; with the
Vichy French against the Allies. An Australian soldier pointed a
gun at me and I put up my hands as fast as they would go. Later
I entered the Lebanese army and patrolled the Palestine border
for a year; but nothing happened. I came home.'

The coldness of the nights spent in the mountains had affected
his eyes, which had filled with blue water. But he remembered
no winter colder than the one past. Each night he was not sure
if he were falling asleep or freezing to death, and wolves had
come down from the north and eaten donkeys in Baaklin.

It was a half-deserted town, like all the countryside, because
its young men emigrated, or worked in Beirut. Early in the
sixteenth century it became the capital of the Druse Maanid
dynasty, the second ruling house of Lebanon, usurping the
Tanuks who had fought against the Crusaders. From Baaklin
the early Maanid princes held the Mountain fitfully against the
Turks, and Fakr ed Din was born here, it is said, in a broken-
down, arcaded building overlooking the glen. The stones of their
palaces show in the façades of other buildings, and a few inscribed
and faded fountains remain. But Fakr ed Din found Baaklin too
arid for his capital, and took the government across the valley to
Deir el Kamar, where the springs were many.

Set on steep hills where pines and olives grow, it is pretty and
intimate, a capital of mountain kings, with erratically-paved
streets which lead away the rain down cobbled gutters.
Maronites and Greek Catholics built churches here a hundred
years ago, crested with belfries, and some Turkish baths lie
among roses. In a fountained square of Umbrian mellowness

Fakr ed Din raised a cloudy-stoned mosque which is still standing, and north of the square are the Kharj barracks, built for his mercenaries, and a dilapidated silk market with arcades and a wide pool. These buildings are strong and handsome, for the prince imported Tuscan architects to design them. Earthquakes, which have ruined half the town, have not affected them, only tilted the mosque's minaret a little, as if the wind bent it.

Fakr ed Din's brother, Yunis al-Maan, built a palace too, and the Tuscans inset it with a doorway of black and yellow stone. During his brother's exile Yunis stood regent for him in the Mountain, and was defeated by Yousuf Safa of Akkar, who was supported by the Turks, and burnt the palaces of Deir el Kamar in 1614. When Fakr returned, he reconciled himself to all his enemies until Yousuf's son came to him, proffering his father's friendship. 'Tell your father, we do not want his present,' he said; 'we want the beams he tore from our palace at Deir el Kamar, which he burnt and destroyed. . . . Does he think to make us forget everything by a present of two horses?'

The Turks, who thought the Safas too powerful, supported Fakr ed Din against them, and he marched his men through hailstorms along the mountains and seized Qalat el Hosn after five days. Soon after, he married one of his daughters to the son of Yousuf Safa, and the vendetta might have ended. But Yousuf, paying his respects to Fakr ed Din and seeing the little emir for the first time asleep on a divan, exclaimed: 'Why, I could tie him to a bunch of keys and put him in my pocket.' And Fakr sprang to his feet in a white rage and rode away, flinging a parchment into the crowds as he left the Safa castle at Akkar:

I am small, but my foes see me great, and stand in awe;
Ye are like the poplar wood; I am the wood's saw. . . . I swear
The stones of Akkar shall build my palace at Deir.

He kept his word, wresting Tripolis from the Safas by cunning, and capturing Akkar soon after. Two ships were sent from Sidon and loaded with the fortress marbles, and its yellow blocks are set in the façades of Deir el Kamar still, and enrich its palace entranceways.

Later in the seventeenth century the Chehabs, descendent from the Maans, held on to Deir el Kamar as the Mountain capital, and it remained so for a hundred and fifty years. They built a palace on the west side of the square, jewelled with a gate of faded stones. A triumvirate of child princes lived here at the end of the eighteenth century and was usurped by the Emir Bechir, who put out their eyes. Their tutor, Juryus Baz, was trapped and executed, but his descendants bought the royal mansions, and own them still.

Nearby is the 'dream house palace' of Pierre Karameh, court poet to Bechir. He is said to have told his master that he had dreamt of entering a palace of his own. So the emir built the palace secretly and bestowed it on him; and it remains a poet's dream: nostalgia of silence and waters, dark with cypresses.

To the south the Chehab emir Melhem built the Grand Seraglio, with a judgement-chamber which has paled into beauty in stones of the yellow Akkar and misted pink and blue. The ministers sat upon a dais while the people stood below, and the emir reclined at the back and smoked when he was bored, under a canopy of intricately-painted wood.

The walls of the courtyard are very tall, and keep its emptiness in a white glare of sun, like a memorial. Twelve hundred Christians of Deir el Kamar were massacred here by the Druses in 1860 and the bullet-holes dimple the stone.

The Druses and Christians had lived together since the time of Fakr ed Din, when the Maronites first edged into southern Lebanon. But after 1840 the friendship dimmed, and when a Druse and a Maronite argued over a partridge which one of them had shot near Deir el Kamar, war broke out and continued intermittingly until 1860, when there were massacres even in Damascus. The Druses, though outnumbered, were disciplined and well-led, and the Turks supported them; but the Christians were disorganized and even called upon their clergy as leaders.

In 1860 the Druses attacked the Christians of Jezzine and the whole population rushed down the ravine where the great river falls, and many hundreds died. Those who reached Sidon were locked outside its walls, and Moslems came from the city and killed them in the flowering orchards, and left their bodies along the sea. There was a massacre at Hasbaya; Zahlé fell. And Deir el Kamar was looted and burnt. Twelve hundred Christians and their families were promised protection by the Turkish governor, who disarmed them and placed them in the great courtyard of the Seraglio, where the Chehabs had once dispensed justice. He did not open the gates for the Druses, but allowed them to enter the courtyard over a low wall. Then the Christian women and children were ordered to separate from the men, and the massacre began. The people of Deir el Kamar still speak about it with bitterness. Lightly they say that the Druses are brothers now, but in other moods they murmur and admit that they keep to themselves.

In 1949 the skeletons were dug up from the court of the Grand Seraglio, now a prison, because the convicts needed a recreation yard. The population, who gathered to watch, said that there were fifteen sackfuls of bones. These were placed in the garden of the Convent of Our Lady of the Mount, behind a marble plaque inscribed with that verse of Ecclesiasticus which prays that the bones of honoured men may live again, and that their name be continued upon their children with glory.

In a wall of the convent, which is modern, lies a stone drawn from some earlier building. It is carved with the emblem of Our Lady of the Mount, patroness of the town, with a pictorial moon below, for Deir el Kamar means 'Monastery of the Moon', which originated, says Burckhardt, 'in a convent which formerly stood here, dedicated to the Virgin, who is generally represented in Syria with the moon beneath her feet'. The moon persists through Middle Eastern worship—balancing the sun-father, the moon-mother; the statues of the Great Goddess, horned with the half-moon. The symbol passed naturally from Astarte to the Virgin. In early ikons she wore the towered crown of Cybele, and her feet rested on the moon's rim. Here the goddess found her gentlest and most human form, as the Divine Mother of a greater Son. Some Arabs still fear and reverence the moon, and counteract its power with amulets and hands, and enamelled eyes of Osiris such as the Phoenicians made. Not long ago farmers were guided by the moon in their times of planting, and in the third or fourth quarter they sowed garden produce and felled timber, because roof-beams which had been cut in the first and second quarters were believed to rot away.

The days I spent in Deir el Kamar were pervaded by the Chamoun family, who lived in a tiny house above a wall-fountain. The father had died, leaving two unmarried sons and a widow who was so emotional and provident that she embodied Lebanese motherhood for me. Myrtle and white roses grew along their courtyard, where insects hung golden at evening. In 1956 the earthquake had shaken their house around them, and the younger brother, Asaad, awoke to find plaster covering his bed, and the stars shining in.

One of their cousins, Camille Chamoun, was President of the Republic, and had cleared away the shacks which masked the palaces of Deir el Kamar, where he had been born. Now by law a house may only be built in the traditional style, out of local limestone, with arcades and double-colonetted windows. This has proved costly for the inhabitants, but their town is harmonious, and it escaped attack during the civil war of 1958, which removed Chamoun from the presidency.

I walked across the valley with Asaad to the palace which Bechir II built when he removed his court from Deir el Kamar. In one of the churches the people were singing the May hymn to the Virgin.

Up the hillside climbed apple-trees in blossom, with dying mulberry groves, grass heavy and damp. Above us, where the palace hid behind a pelmet of walls, we saw a flight of seventy or eighty storks which pass like clockwork every spring and autumn between Russia and Cairo. And I remembered that two and a half millennia ago Herodotus had seen this too, and written that they fly every year, with just precision, between Scythia and the Upper Nile, beating their silent wings against the sun.

We took the carriage-way which Bechir built between Beit-ed-din and Deir el Kamar, one of the first roads in the land, while 'the Alhambra of Lebanon' remained secret above, and a castle rose behind us on a plume of trees. We passed a kiosk built for one of the emir's sons, where cypresses had stood, each one so large that three men could not link hands around it; and we reached the ruined palace mill, under which the water ran now with a hollow, intestinal mocking, and the millstones were broken like crusts of bread.

But inside the palace the Moorish dream dies. Here is an empty *meidan*, where the emir Bechir held horse-games and court barbecues and received Ibrahim Pasha of Egypt. The inner palace is reached by the 'Tumbling Stairs', down which an over-important pasha was once butted by a stray sheep. The steps are worn and shadowed underfoot. An inlaid gate is entered, an iron-shod doorway passed. And we stood in the Grand Court, seeing arches and terraces in tiers of coloured masonry, tall, barred windows and balustraded stairs. But the courtyard does not surround; it confronts. Against its unyielding whiteness scarcely a flower or grass-blade moves, though a few trees or plants could have been placed here more easily than the arduously chiselled slabs, and softened art with nature.

In the Alhambra the Moors understood this union, befriended water and abducted sunlight into their courts and myriad ceilings.

And the Damascenes, whose styles were copied by Bechir, knew how a group of lemon trees could soften and transform hard surfaces with colour and shadow.

It is the incidents of the palace which give most pleasure: small courts where creepers fall, the long pool of the poets' academy, and the Moorish baths, which let the sun in as a forest does, spreading the marbled floor with pastel lights. But the gardens are closed behind lattice doors, rather formal and Victorian, except where the tomb of the emir's first wife, Sitt es-Chams, lies in a sheaf of cypresses.

In the doors and halls, the mosaic and marble, the arabesques and painted woods, were executed by craftsmen from Damascus after the style of their city. The decorated ceilings, which grow oppressive when neglected, are kept lustrous and superb, but the paint has faded from many mouldings, showing their poverty, and sometimes the inlay, in its small way, is flamboyant. It is this ornateness, and the relegation of flowers and trees to formal splendour, which suggest that Beit-ed-din was built for the self-enhancement of which an Arab is still specially conscious. Asaad spoke of Bechir's time as *Le Grand Siècle*, and so it was, but there was a puff of decadence too, an empty bravura.

As a junior member of the Chehab family Bechir took the throne from his cousins and was twice displaced before he blinded and imprisoned them. Quick and subtle and sometimes cold-hearted, he ruled with justice when he could, and allied himself to Mehemet Ali against the Turks. Privately a Christian, he governed without bias as Fakr ed Din had done, and kept the fast of Ramadhan and the muezzin's call to prayer. When his first wife died, he took a Circassian slave-girl, fifteen years old, forced her to become Christian by threatening to send her to the kitchens, and married her secretly in a chapel at Beit-ed-din. One of her dresses, miasmically embroidered and turned into a chasuble, hangs in the palace museum.

For a time Bechir was friendly with Lady Hester, but later she harboured his fugitive enemies at Joun, and he tried to intimidate her by murdering her servants. But with a mace above her head and a knife under her pillow she slept soundly, and said that 'if he sent his son to make terms with her she would gladly kill him with her own hands'.

Every winter he passed his falconers in review before him in the mountains, and waited at a vantage point while two thousand peasants beat the valleys; and as soon as he cast his falcon, sixty courtiers on silk-covered horses would gallop down the mountains behind a cloud of dogs, to deprive the bird of the royal game.

Bechir spent thirty years in building, believing that as long as his palace was unfinished his power would be ascendant. Visitors received into the Great Reception Room found themselves standing on a marble floor, facing a long chamber where chandeliers dripped from heavy, splendid ceilings. Secretaries crouched before silver inkstands, and black slaves stood mute and watchful, their sashes stuck with pistols and Damascus swords. At the back of the room, framed in stained glass under a painted canopy, Bechir sat on his heels, almost hidden in the smoke which rose from a huge bowl before him. A cashmere shawl was bound over his forehead above, a tuft of brows, and behind his waist-length beard the diamond pommel of a dagger glittered. His voice, when he at last spoke, was cavernous, like an oracle, and through the smoke the eyes were glinting and terrible. This appearance alone wreaked havoc among enemies, and it was said that in anger his beard stood up on end like a lion's mane, but that when he saw that he had frightened a man, he would repent and speak reassuringly.

Burckhardt was a guest in the palace before its completion, and Lamartine has a room and a valley named after him. He saw five hundred horses stabled in the great *meidan*, with laden camels, and says that behind a barred arcade a tiger slept. The *meidan* is bare, but in the museum which flanks it the costumes and arms of *Le Grand Siècle* have been preserved: the long pelisses and heavy-buckled sashes of the harem, the silver tantour headdress* and the lace veil; prophylactic charms encased in necklaces; and a waxwork emir, turbaned like a mushroom and dangling a low-slung sabre. In one vitrine is a Russian sword presented to the emir by Napoleon during the siege of Acre; and nearby, in a gallery of documents, I found a blunt letter from Palmerston, refusing to help Bechir after the fall of Mehemet Ali: '. . . you will have to take the consequences . . .' And the consequences were the exile of Bechir in Constantinople, where he died in 1850, the abolition of the Lebanese monarchy, and the setting up of fragmentary states. But not long ago the remains of the emir were brought back from

* The tantour was the distinctive headdress for women in the Mountain, but died out in the middle of the nineteenth century; it was like the mediaeval steeple headdress, with pendent veil and horn, sometimes two feet high (the height depending on the woman's station) and slightly tapering.

Istanbul to the mountains and buried with his first wife in the tomb in the English gardens.

The palace passed to the governor of Lebanon and is still the summer residence of the president, who sits in the *liwan* of the harem on hot evenings beside a mother-of-pearl encrusted stool, with a telephone.

*   *   *

Wazeem was a goatherd whom I had met near Beit-ed-din and who lived in the village of Simkaniye, a clump of houses concealed among apple trees. He had a wife with strange light eyes, and eight children who all fitted into one room for the night, while I slept in another and a goat occupied the third. A strong house, with wrought-iron windows, they had built it from government money after the earthquake, and they now looked over to the streaked folds of the Barouk mountains, and felt the morning sun.

Wazeem could not read at all, but Rames, his eldest son, was eighteen and still at school. While Wazeem walked in *cheroual* pantaloons, taking his goats to market through the hills, and his wife carried the Druse *mandil*, Rames wore a shabby suit and was always reciting *Julius Caesar*. With his small body, and precocious head stacked in boyish hair, he looked like T. E. Lawrence, and it was hard to believe that he was not very clever. The resonance of the English language drugged him, and he would repeat Mark Antony's speeches to himself in a reverential chant. What was the difference between Portia and Calpurnia, he asked; and what was Cassius really like? And at meals he would murmur absent-mindedly ' "You blocks, you stones . . ." ' or ' "Knew you not Pompey?" '

But these were mythic figures to him, characters Shakespeare had invented; he did not know that Pompey seized the Middle East for Rome and slew brigands in the Lebanese hills, nor that Cassius had withdrawn the broken legions of Crassus from Parthia to the west. Shakespeare and Milton were more real. Thumbing through my passport Rames saw that one of my names was Dryden and lapsed into *Alexander's Feast* and asked me to stay with him a month to teach him better English. How great was the tribe of Dryden, he asked, and where was its village?

I had to confess that the tribe was small.

He said that we should increase it by heavy breeding. This was why his father had eight children: to enlarge the Druse nation. 'Dryden was great,' he said, and I felt that I had lapsed in my responsibilities.

In a year Rames hoped to study aircraft engineering and go to England. He might have taught literature, but 'Shakespeare', he said, 'can't make you money', and money and position were obsessive, filling the one dimension of his mind. A man must escape the frustration of village life; he may return to see his family, who are always loved, but he must live and advance somewhere else.

Wazeem was the last of his world, and watched his son with proud, bewildered eyes, as if down an avenue. And when Rames goes away, they will pin his photograph on the wall and Wazeem will say, 'My son is an aircraft engineer in ——. *Yullah!* He is earning ——. Yes, really. More than the goats could get in ten years. God is merciful!' And the mother will sigh.

Almost every mother in Lebanon keeps this pain in her. When a guest is present the men scarcely acknowledge her. She moves in and out like an old servant, her feet copiously slippered, her tread softer than falling leaves. From time to time she calls 'Welcome!' and 'Eat!' and brings houmous and eggs and olives. 'Goat's milk is refreshing.' 'You are like another son.' And suddenly, as if caught by a physical ache, she sighs and looks down. 'Is your mother not sad for you so far away? Does she not fear? God bring you back to her!'

God, to the Druses, is a force, a pervasive unity. 'Thus is the figure of the Almighty', run the creeds; 'it does not eat, nor drink, nor feel, nor can incidents of time alter it. It is invisible, but contains the power of being ever present. . . .' And it is this Unknowable which the Druse invokes, like an orthodox Moslem, without question or imagination.

For Rames' mother the time of loss had not yet come. The house was like an orphanage. At night the frogs strummed outside, while from the room next door came whimpers and sighs and shreds of dreams. I wondered if their nights were always like this, or if my arrival had disturbed the children. I was the first foreigner the little ones had seen. They would sit and stare up at me like worshippers before an idol, and I thought how years later they might retrieve from early memories the European who came to their house, stooping under a pack, and slept on their divan. And momentarily it seemed a sacrilege to pass through this alchemy of childhood remembrance, which softens and illumines, and holds its fragments bright and precious to the eye, as if to make amends for all the past that it forgets.

The family rose at four o'clock and ate the Mountain breakfast of bread dipped in sweet milk. In the dawn the children sat out on the verandah with their mother; and their blondness and the woman's haunting eyes seemed spun from the young light.

Early travellers, seeing this pale beauty in the Druses, thought they must be Europeans. Others wrote that they were a lost tribe of Israel, fled from the wrath of Moses when he broke the Golden Calf; or Ituraeans, whom Pompey quelled; or Hindus or Hittites or Samaritans; and already there were rumours of their Iranian and Mesopotamian origin: a Cuthite tribe transplanted by Esarhaddon, or the Derusaiaioi, whom Herodotus said had been moved by Cyrus from Media.

But oddest and most persistent was the tale that they were the remnant of Crusaders, followers of the Comte de Dreux who had marched his men into the mountains after the fall of Acre. The grey-eyed children, tangled in the sun, lent their approval to the moment's vision. One or two were dark and small and might have been heirs to Norman baronies; but the rest could come of Gallic or Saxon stock, and the oldest girl, with her heart-shaped face, was perhaps of Provence. The Queen of Jerusalem sat spinning on her balcony, her *mandil* wound about her like a wimple, while the lords of Antioch and Edessa chased each other through the orchards with oil-cans. The seignories of the Holy Land preserved a fragile peace, until a princess of Tripolis dropped a bunch of thistles on the Grand Master of the Teutonic Knights, who burst into tears.

Rames came out, apologized for the children and chased them indoors. He had to go to school, and I to Mouchtara, and for a moment we walked down the road until, in his shy, abrupt manner, he said good-bye. After a detour through olive trees I found the road, and looking back for a moment, saw the wimpled queen alone on her verandah, spinning in the sun.

8. The Goodly Mountain

> I pray thee, let me go over, and see
> the good land that is beyond Jordan,
> that goodly mountain, and Lebanon.
> *Deuteronomy iii. 25*

THE SEARCH FOR A GODDESS offers no plain direction. Clothed by nature and history, she is pervasive but intangible, stands in ruined temples, and rustles underfoot. Her identity, as the ancients knew it, has been found in Tyre and Sidon, and the mountain people remember her in the Holy Mother and keep her shrines on the high places.

But the old view of life has gone. Religion now asks men to discipline their instincts or to ignore them, while the Phoenicians saw that nature's blood was their own. And it was because of this, because they asked to be free, that the Greeks raised the goddess to the sphere of love.

The mystery is like the circles from a stone, which flow out over a lake. Early man, who kindled fire and thought it to have come from spirits, later grew familiar with it, and forgot that it was divine. He looked up and found god in the sun, and afterwards, discovering this god to be a globe of incandescent gas, he groped into the abstract. Wherever his comprehension rules, there can be no sanctity.

Yet as I walked through Lebanon, the Phoenician view became more real. Man is distinguished from the rest of nature by his mind, and the Phoenician mind, for all his achievements, was scarcely yet awake. There must have been comfort in the scale and durability of nature, when the rivers came down from holy groves in the pale mountains, running to the sea for ever, while the camel-trains shuffled and died along them: Amorites, Arameans, Hittites.

Long after, the Druses owned the southern mountains and the Barouk river, and have left ruined mills knee-high in anemones against its banks. The Jumblatts came from Aleppo early in the seventeenth century and built palaces in the hills, and lost their Kurdish blood among the Druses. Early in the eighteenth century they crushed the Druse Arslans in battle, and a hundred years later were able to face Bechir with twenty thousand men on the plain of Simkaniye.

In their new palace at Mouchtara, 'The Chosen Place', they turned at bay, and Bechir reduced them by guile, sending an *'uqqal* with a peace treaty, while he moved up his army. As the Jumblatt bey took the paper from the *'uqqal*'s hand, he looked up and saw the hills above the Barouk river dark with soldiers. The palace was abandoned for the passes of Jezzine and the Beqaa, and Bechir stopped his forces at its gates to protect the Jumblatt women. But when the bey died by the bowstring, Bechir returned and tore up the marble pavements of Mouchtara and carried them to Beit-ed-din.

The Jumblatts are still the most powerful of the Druses, and their bey is a parliamentary deputy and a socialist. He has given away part of his ancestral estate, and the property at Mouchtara is divided among his family. Grown from the hill squarely, the palace keeps its oriel windows and moulded doors. There is a frivolous Italianate wing where a Jumblatt sister spends her summers, reached by a horseshoe stairway of falling marble steps. But within, the palace is without style or order. The emir Bechir left it in aristocratic decay, but later Jumblatts restored it after a puffy European taste, and this too has deteriorated, leaving the rooms gaunt.

I walked under a sculptured lion, which held an electric bulb in its mouth, and up some stairs to the palace centre, where Kamel Jumblatt Bey lives. The bey was absent, but a porter led me to the kitchens, where servants lay asleep in a feudal gloom. The apartments of Kamel Bey were ranged about a restored courtyard, open on the south where the mountains stood thunder-blue. In one room hung photographs of Ghandi and Nasser, and a picture of the bey's mother, 'the Veiled Lady of Mouchtara', who had possessed something of the influence and awesomeness of Lady Hester. There was almost nothing of value: a moulded eagle, a marble fountain-head, some rusty sabres.

A servant offered to show me the gardens. He was awaiting reprisal in a vendetta, and wore a pistol strapped to his thigh. I told him I was English and he rubbed his fingers together in a gesture of concord, for there is a belief that the English are reincarnated Druses.

The early Jumblatts cut passages through the hills and brought the Barouk waters to their terraces, where the walks were once cloudy with lilac, and tendrils of water reflected many roses. A cupola still stands, with some kingly cypress trees, but the rest is not tended, and beauty has gone.

I sat in a bare hall while the servants brought me a meal fit, at least, for a socialist prince, then squatted on divans to watch me eat. Later they offered me a room, and in the morning allowed me to go without the usual breakfast of bread and sweet milk.

I wandered toward the Barouk mountains past many family tombs of the Druses; through Ain Qaniye, half of whose villagers live in a Jumblatt palace; and Amatour, with its delicately carved and weathered doors, once a proud town through whose streets no foreigner might ride his horse and no prisoner be led manacled. At Baadaran I saw an abandoned palace, the Druse lions still rampant in its stone and the walls untouched, and climbed to a tableland where the Barouk ranges rolled treeless one against the other, and swelled in whiteness far to the north, like a brush-stroke on the sky.

High above Maaser-es-Chouf the cedars are a cloud's shadow. From this grove, the largest in Lebanon, Solomon may have received the wood for his temple, for 'Solomon sent to Huram the king of Tyre, saying, As thou didst deal with David my father, and didst send him cedars to build him an house to dwell therein, even so deal with me. . . . Send me also cedar trees, fir trees, and algum trees, out of Lebanon: for I know that thy servants can skill to cut timber in Lebanon; and behold, my servants shall be with thy servants, even to prepare me timber in abundance: for the house which I am about to build shall be wonderful great.'*

The Tyrian woodsmen may have cut the forest on the east side of the peak and rolled the cedars down into the Litani river, floating them to the sea a few miles north of Tyre; 'and we will bring it to thee in floats by sea to Joppa; and thou shalt carry it up to Jerusalem'.

Through biblical, classical and Arab times the trees were felled for ships and dwellings. The earth eroded and the rain washed it away, leaving grey rock where the plants were killed in infancy by goats. As the forests dwindled they grew more precious, and the copse of Maaser-es-Chouf, though not exceeding four hundred big trees, is the largest which remains.

It was at Maaser that I met Yusef Haddad. 'Those are the true cedars of the Lord.' He spoke with awe and reverence, but in English with an American accent. 'I remember loads of foxes

* II Chronicles ii. 3, 8, 9.

and hyenas there when I was a kid, with wolves and bears sometimes, and wild pig. But you see nothing now. Animals gone away to work in Beirut, I guess, like everybody else.'

He himself had gone away more than sixty years before and had found work in Connecticut where he had passed his young manhood. Thousands of Lebanese have done the same, and though some have returned, they are subtly different, and recognize the change in themselves. Most Arabs live with an emotional immediacy and are, I believe, less complex and various than Europeans, contrary to the romantic view. But being receptive, they may alter quickly. The émigré returned from a well-developed country is unmistakably poised and softened.

Now almost eighty, Yusef lived in the house which his family had always owned. There was a tradition among the Haddads that they were once blacksmiths in Damascus—for 'haddad' means 'smith'—and that they had fled to the Hauran after Tamerlane sacked the city in 1400, and entered the mountains. Yusef did not know that Damascus had been famous for its smiths and armourers, nor that the art of forging Damascus blades, which declined after the Mongols left, might have died with his people in the Hauran. But he said that he could trace back his line five hundred years, and had pinned up the Smith pedigree in one of his rooms: a pictorial tree in whose trunk sat the first-known forefather, turbaned, lugubrious and sprouting many labelled leaves, of which Yusef was one.

The village of Maaser partly belonged to the Druses. Twice in the nineteenth century they had plundered his family, and in the 1860 massacres his grandfather had been killed as he carried the Christian flag against them at Zahlé.

When Yusef was fifteen a friend bought a ticket to America, but decided not to leave. 'I told my father that if he didn't give me the money for the ticket I'd run away. There wasn't nothing to do here; just feedin' silkworms. So my poor father bought that ticket and I took the boat with the papers under the other guy's name. His brother came to meet him at the New York docks and was kinda furious to find me there instead. So I hit Danbury, Connecticut, after forty days, and went around selling holy pictures. I caught malaria and tried my hand at ice-cutting one summer, and got a job pulling the hair off rabbits' skins for women's hats. Silly kinda business.'

He remembered all the names and dates. 'After that I left Danbury for Waterbury—everything's something-bury over that way—and I ended up with three groceries and a barber's shop. I had no education, you see, and I had to build myself. And so I did. And then I got married.'

His wife was over seventy now, but neat and pretty as a bird. She had been born in Maaser too, but had lived on the other side of the village. Her parents had forced her into an engagement with the village tailor, whom she did not love, and when he emigrated to Waterbury he took her with him as his fiancée. Here she met Yusef and they married in the French church.

Her gentle face and the heavy, wise features of Yusef seemed to blend. They reminded me of my own father and mother. He was strength and she was sweetness. There was no bitterness in either, though here and there a regret. Illness had hounded Yusef most of his life. He grew sick as his business prospered, and doctors in New Haven, Denver and New York examined him without discovering the cause. 'So I returned to Maaser, where the village doctor saw that I had an abscess, as if he had been right there inside me. And I went to the Beirut hospital where they punctured my spine in the wrong place and left my foot as stiff as old chewing-gum, like you see it now. I was in and out of bed for twelve years, but afterwards God came and stopped the pain.'

Now he walked down the alleys of Maaser with a stick, and swung his leg before him. All his talk and movements were ripe and zestful. He was not old at all. Shielded from the sun by a Hollywood stetson, he would go to see his nephew, who had also been to the States and wore a Californian wide-brimmed hat. They would sit over a backgammon board outside a café, and mingled with the old Arab cries of 'Aiwah!' and 'Yullah!' the watching villagers would hear a Martian dialogue:

'I gotcha cornered.'

'Yeah?'

'You gone an' bust me with a double.'

He showed me the church, whose illumination was two hundred and twenty candle-power strong, and 'I reckon that's the brightest in this territory.' The lights flashed on, battery after battery, until the saints seemed to blink and cringe on the ikonostasis. And instead of giving a candle to the Virgin one could switch on six or seven rows of bulbs in front of her, and make an offering towards the electricity bill. There had been a church here before, built early in the seventeenth century, 'shortly before I was born', said Yusef; but it had decayed. The Druse population of Maaser was expanding more quickly than the Christian, and to consolidate their community they collected money from émigrés and relations, received a donation from the Pope, and built a convent with their own hands.

Yusef was never still. He was adding rooms to his own house and his wife wanted chickens—'A house is empty without a chicken in it.' They could remember when every family was self-sufficient, owning its own wheat and cows and chickens. A sheep bought at the beginning of the year, and killed before winter, would last through the next year. Now wheat and mutton came from Australia and Syria. They had not seen a cow for years, and there were only three goats in the village. The people lived by their apple harvest or their olives.

There was a time when the coast could not be reached except by tracks, and people who had fallen sick had to be trussed on donkeys and taken over the hills to Beirut. Yusef had said that the village must have a road, and one Sunday everybody left church with picks and shovels and started to build it, and linked Maaser with the highway to Beit-ed-din in two and a half years. He and his wife grew poor again because of his illness, but he bought a barren hillock to the south of the village and imported vines from Italy and worked for fifteen years until the soil bore fruit.

'The hill is steep and difficult; every eight feet we had to build a terrace. But it is only the rocks which spoil the farming here.' He held up the palms of his creased hands in a gesture of fruitfulness. 'The soil is rich, if only you plough it.'

They did not know if they would be able to return to the United States, but the stetson hung in the passageway and they poured their arak from an American whiskey bottle. Everything they had gained they had made with their own hands, from striving. Their world was real and whole, grown up from strength, year after year, like the cedars above them.

*　　　*　　　*

As I climbed into the mountains, Druse women came onto their rooftops in the village below, clasping their long veils in their hands as they pointed me the path; and by this graceful semaphore I reached the road to the cedars.

Clouds moved along the rim of the mountain, as if the wind chafed the snow there. And the goddess signified her presence in a shadow of rich trees, strangely compact and solitary.

Hiram's men were few among many who laid the Mountain bare. For two millennia the Egyptians had been building with the cedars of Byblos, and the Romans cut the forest of Kadisha for their navies, and the Byzantines after them.

For thirty years the people of the district have deprived themselves of goats so that the young trees might rise un-molested from the stones. At this age they stand straight and tapering-armed, and aspire to the sky; but as they grow older their boles multiply and their branches swell across the earth, compacting to a shelf-like beauty. I measured the largest of the grove, and found it to be almost fifty feet around its trunk, some two thousand years old, grown from the rocks like a limb of the world. Wherever the enormous shadows fell, the grass was like a lawn, and trembled with mauve flowers.

The mountain people venerate the cedars. Not long ago they thought the trees half human. The height at which they grow, their silence and loneliness, deepened their mystique. They seemed to hold council. And as I walked among the older cedars I saw that two altars, carved with crosses and the symbolic moon, had been built there, where people come to pray and to hold Mass.

The simplicity of the altars placed among the majesty of the trees made light of time. The silence in those strange aisles, the windless sky and the god's-eye view of streams and mountains were old in holiness. A prayer or chant could echo here in touch with every age, the blood and flesh be poured for any god.

*   *   *

I came down through galleries of stubborn snow to Barouk, whose villagers were once brigands and gamblers, and plundered corn from the peasants of Beqaa. Through its valley Antiochus the Great forced a bloodless passage in 219 B.C., following the road from Heliopolis to Sidon against the Ptolemies, and left his heavy infantry beneath the valley fortresses, to enter Tyre in triumph.

The Barouk valley is ledgy with rocks where farmers have wrestled with the hills, and lost. I passed Ain Zhalta by the Damour; cedars on the peaks above, like moss on stone. And at evening I saw the Beirut–Damascus road, the waist of Lebanon, and looked north to the highest mountains, mingled with bright ranges of clouds along their whole length.

The hotels in the hills stay closed until summer, but I found one which was being demolished and which offered me a room, where I stayed with a small, discoloured cat. It was already mid-May, but the clouds rolled up from the sea every morning and covered the land until night. We dwelt in twilight, the cars groping along the road, flicking their headlights at one another, and cloud entered the broken hotel like a mist. At night verminous shadows fled across the rubble when I opened my door, and the cat howled.

'I wish you'd stop feeding the cat,' the proprietor called to me. 'If you feed a cat it won't catch anything.'

I pointed out the similarity in size between the cat and its prey; if it were not fed it would not grow; and since the hotel was being demolished it did not matter anyway.

He answered that not all the hotel was coming down; they were renovating. Would I please let the cat hunt? Had I never owned one?

'Yes,' I said, and did not tell him that my cat had died of being overfed. But after three days the demolishers began tapping at the wall of my room, which exuded beetles, and I left for the mountains.

It thundered in the afternoon and the rain fell steadily, cleaning the clouds from the hills. I sheltered in a workshop where an old carpenter was chiselling wood and chuckling to himself. He took me to his home and his wife said that I looked like her son. Their son had gone away to Africa and had sent home many wooden Masai warriors, and though the old man was doubtful of their craftsmanship, he had set them up around the cottage.

Mount Sannin filled the windows of the house, ascending with a massive assuredness on the shoulders of the peaks around it, a first among equals. Along the way the flood-waters fell from every fissure of the rock, until at Kfar Selouan the road became a track. Usually I passed almost unnoticed through the villages, since nobody expected that a foreigner would be walking. But as I approached Kfar Selouan a troop of boys saw me. Children tumbled out of houses and ran in from the fields, so that I entered with more than fifty of them behind me, to the astonishment of a group of old men, who wondered if it were a religious procession. The children told me that the road to Sannin was blocked with snow, and grinned.

'Knee-deep.'

'Waist-high.'

'You could drown.'

A wan, serious youth said that it might be possible to cross the mountain. 'But you would need a whole day, and the sun is falling. Come with me. My father is in Baghdad, but my mother and grandfather are at home.'

His mother was young. She blended a European ease with Arab emotionalism, and was most womanly. Many members of the family came and went, but I remember Youmna best, who was pretty in the fulsome Arab way, with lustrous hair and a rich voice. She said that there was an altar on the Kniseh mountain above us, with ancient stones; but the snow still covered the summit, and nobody knew when it would melt, the weather was so strange. She had even seen a bear in the village that winter.

A pile of cushions had been placed in a corner of the room with blankets and a tray of olives, and amongst these the grandfather lay. He was not ill, but his legs would only support him for a few yards, so he remained in the darkness; a wasted Byzantine figure who sometimes smiled. Looking at his face, I felt that life was not being extinguished, but was sliding away. It flickered back and forth within his eyes. Often he lay silent, his ikonic hands against the floor. The world's urgency had palled and his abstraction laid a gentle scorn on it. Then the light would quicken and he would peer up beneath wispy eyebrows, and ask if the British were still in Aden, or whether I found the Lebanon beautiful. In the evening he raised himself into a chair in the candlelight and at night, while his family slept, his shadow still wavered on the wall, its arms crossed on its chest like a Theban king, staring into nothing.

Morning came with bells. The family wanted me to join them at Mass, so we all climbed to the church, except for the old man, who was observing the ancient rite of breakfast. The Maronites keep their liturgy in Syriac—Aramaic, the language of Christ—and are the only church to do so; but some villages, like Kfar Selouan, mingle this with Arabic. The men and women divided, as in a mosque; the compact, grizzled farmers in front, their woollen caps still on their heads; the half-veiled women behind.

Beneath his shiny skull the priest's beard frothed and dissolved into a snowy chasuble, so that whiteness clothed him to the floor and his head moved independently above it, as if he were trans-figured. From time to time the pageant of Mass was inter-rupted. The chanters, bandying Arabic and Syriac between them, were hesitant, and one soloist anticipated his cue.

'No-no-no,' said the priest. 'Not you.'

And once his eyes grew stern through the incense. 'You must not sleep during the divine service,' he said; and an ancient in the front pew started and looked crestfallen.

*   *   *

At first the track over Sannin led through pinnacles of watered rock, which the shepherds call 'ghosts'. Then the snow covered it in flat curves and lunettes, parting before small, damp meadows where crocuses and lilies grew, delicate on the mountain's strength. One by one the peaks lifted themselves around me: the zebra mass of Hermon; Zarour to the west, bony and luminous; and the Barouk ranges in the south, over whose crest Yusef had climbed as a child to pick mulberry-leaves for silk-worms, bringing them back still moist before dawn.

Sannin was all clarity and bareness; the only sound the flowing of water under the snow-fields. From here the great Beqaa valley spreads wrinkled through the hills. On the other side the Dog River falls steep and hidden to the sea, and the road to Damascus shows as a ridge, where the Roman camels carried silk to Berytus and went back into Chalcis with linen and sweet wine. Ituraea, Canaan, Naphtali, all the wounded hills and valleys— and on a clear day you may see Cyprus, where ships of Tarshish dropped their silver anchors, and brought Adonis to the island kings.

9. Cold Flowing Waters

Will a man leave the snow of
Lebanon which cometh from the rock
of the field? Or shall the cold flowing
waters be forsaken?

Jeremiah xviii. 14

SPRING HAD PASSED INTO SUMMER. The heat rebounded
from the rocks, leaving the country dazzled and spent. On the
lower mountains the snow died and the peasants who still
worked on the terraces seemed to be dreaming, their minds
stunned in the forge of the sun.

Toward noon I would find an orchard and lapse into sleep,
until the sun shone under the fruit trees. But the nights were
cold and I was afraid to leave my fire bright, but nestled among
rocks and doubled the sleeping-bag round me. Viewed from the
hills, the sun's rise was joyous and purposeful in the pure sky,
and each evening its fall brought sudden winds as it was lost in a
smear of blood behind the sea.

In the identification of light with life, which belongs to all
religions, the Phoenicians linked Adonis with the sun. Each dusk
he went to his death at the rim of the world and at dawn ascended
to Astarte. But the diffusion and complexity of their belief lent
it many variants. Studying the skies as the Babylonians had, they
saw that in summer the sun passed through the upper hemisphere
in the sign of the Bull, where the moon finds her zenith and the
planet Venus shines, worshipped by ancient Semites as Astarte.
But in winter the sun descended to the lower world and entered
Scorpio, the sign of Mars, who killed him, and perhaps it was
from this that the Phoenicians saw Mars as a destroyer.

The concept of redemption remained linked with the sun. The
first Christians faced the east to pray, and called their Redeemer
the 'Sun of Righteousness', and Sunday became the Lord's day
as heir to a long Mithraic cult. When He died the sun was
extinguished, as it had been for Buddha and for Caesar, and as it
would be again for Charlemagne; and although it is not written
in the Gospels that Christ descended into darkness before His
resurrection, this soon became a dogma.

So the older customs lingered, as they had done in all preceding changes. But Christians refused to see man any more as a toy of the elements, and gave him rebirth in God, a new spirit. For the Phoenicians there was no such renewal, and a slighter morality. God was not so much a judge and saviour as an explanation. He did not die for men's sins, but died in the very order of things, because destruction was a part of nature, and for the same reason was reborn.

Spring, which signalled this rebirth, faded from the hills. Suddenly the nights were warm and pale with a scimitar moon, and many hamlets, almost invisible by day, sprinkled lights along the Dog valley. The whole flow of life changed with the season and was slack and aimless. I spent three days indolently with a village barber and his family near where the river, in its childhood, runs down from Sannin. The barber's wife spoke quietly in French, and came of a family of poets. She had a small daughter with sultana eyes and Victorian ringlets, who wanted to come back to England with me in my rucksack, and there was a grandmother who would walk round a path in the early morning to peep over the window of my room and would be betrayed by a wisp of hair above the ledge; and when I looked out she would smile elfishly and ask me to eat raw broad-beans with her, or drink coffee. She knew how to bake mountain-bread, slapping the dough between her forearms until she could spread it thinly. The villagers' ovens are curved iron plates, heated from below with sticks, and the bread is peeled off in huge circles, thin and mottled. When the French first came to Lebanon, she said, they found these pieces of bread neatly folded beside their plates, mistook them for table-napkins and tied them round their necks.

I went north into Kesrouan, to the highest tributaries of the Dog River, where Maronites plant cherry and apple trees. They were lonely villages, whose people were anxious to know the purpose of my journey and why I did not fear the wild beasts which they imagined to flourish in all districts but their own.

I remember only one sad person, a small girl with a face already old. Each time she approached her mother, smiling, she was met with eyes which did not understand, and it must have been for this that little lines depressed her mouth into a widow's scowl. But she went on trying, running her hands along her mother's knees, and each time they were brushed away the coldness grew in her face.

Normally the mountain people are kind to their children and dote on their babies. But in other ways the pattern is not sure. They are not cruel, but sometimes lack imagination, the spring of tenderness. I once found a crowd of children who were watching a butcher kill a calf. If they understood that it was afraid, they accepted this as natural, and without nervousness or gloating merely looked, with the same brown eyes as the calf, and saw the red fountain from its throat, unmoved.

Men's talk is often of abstracts, but the boundaries of imagination are sharply drawn. 'There is nothing to see there; just stones,' said a family as I left them for a Roman ruin. 'Like Baalbec, only smaller. Stay with us another day.' And the warmth of their invitation and the apparent uselessness of the stones were an embarrassment to me.

It is a comment on the grandeur of the Roman Empire that one may walk along an empty valley and find the ruins of a whole town whose name is unknown. Qalat Fakra, as the Arabs call it, was raised on a ridge above the high tributaries of the Dog, where the Kesrouan mountains fall away. The rocks sprout vertically from the hills, their edges sharpened by erosion, falling in wrinkles as if a throng of headless statues stood there with their hands folded beneath their robes.

Among them the city mounts the hill in rock-cut steps, starred with wild tulips, and farmers have sown apple trees nearby and shored up their terraces with engraved blocks. An enclosure of bossed stones was once a temple to Atargatis, 'the Syrian Goddess' of Lucian, who reigned in eastern Syria with the qualities of Astarte. Later Arabs used her sanctuary as a fortress and ran a palisade around its rim, and beside it the Byzantines built a small church with a raised apse and a nave of ten columns.

Higher on the hill are natural labyrinths of wafery rock, where tombs were cut; and from them grows a fawn-stoned façade, lightly moulded with pilasters and lined by a broken portico. This, cradled in stones and half open to the sky, is a temple to Adonis. Its walls merge with the rock. Half the columns of its courtyard are erect, with clumsy double pillars at the corners and a carved god, disguised by his decay, still rigid on a console.

The temple cella lies beyond wide steps and the plinths of overthrown columns; when these were upright and the sanctuary walls rose plain and heavy behind, worshippers must have entered with awe. There is still a Doric austerity about it, a sense of the absolute, but the arrangement of the temple—the

[93]

shrine within the courtyard—is Semitic, and its simplicity and blunt strength are more Phoenician than classical. The search is not for beauty but for the power of the elder gods. The temple might have grown with the mountains, and around it the folding ridges of the wild-sown rocks seem sculptured with scarcely less intention than pillars and walls.

The Roman road, still fitfully paved, enters the city where a tower is raised twenty-one feet out of buff stone, and roofed by a step-pyramid which could be seen for many miles. In an angle of its walls a Greek inscription says that it was built in the year 355 of the Seleucid era—A.D. 43—'to the Greatest God'; and over its entrance some worn letters dedicate it to the Emperor Claudius. Because the inscriptions are not specific, the purpose of the tower is unknown, though it has been called a monument in honour of Claudius, or a municipal tomb. But the 'Greatest God' was a synonym of Adonis, and the tower's mouldings and construction are like those of the temple nearby, and of a tower which I saw later in the heart of the Adonis cult.

The stairway drew me up in darkness. There was a smell of stagnant water. The light came old and misty through slit windows and recesses, filtered round angles in the passages. The walls were inset with niches, too small for graves. And as the tower could be entered by two doors, so it offered two stairways to the roof. Whoever took the first would emerge within the pyramid, while the second climbed into sunlight and entered the roof chamber by a way still gaping in the fallen stones.

This dual character pervades the tower. The movements of a person inside could be watched and guided from above by priests, if such they were, access given or denied to other rooms, light inducted and shut off. The mystery, the esoteric niches, the maze, seem to have been calculated, like the ascent through Osirian darkness into light. They reminded me of the words of Lucian, who mentions with tantalizing brevity 'the secret rites of Adonis', and of those 'Tombs of Adonis' which appear to have been scattered through his sacred country.

There were grooves in the tower where doors had swung, and signs of other passages broken away. A sunken central chamber could be reached past a sliding door, controlled from the roof above, so that a man might be barred from it or isolated inside. Nobody has found an explanation for this planned confusion, but it may be that here, during the mourning for the dead Adonis, his image was laid in state until the women, following

[94]

an old ritual, came weeping to the sepulchre and found him resurrected, as they did once for that other God in Judaea.

*   *   *

I camped in the mazes of Qalat Fakra, where the Byzantine columns clustered like daffodils and the Roman road spread directionless. The graceful, useless pillars and arcane debris of walls were no longer as their architects imagined them, but products of chance survival. Everything functional and animate, the warmth and complexities, the flow of life was lost. One would like to love not ruins, but what they represent. Yet over the years their forms have been broken down, and now a new aesthetic intrudes. From the columns which posture against the clouds it is hard to build a temple in the mind. They keep a sheer romance about them; and one is beguiled by their new beauty, persuaded that what is poignant now was splendid then, drugged by their waning stones and the peace of the flower-growing earth.

I fell asleep expecting to wake to the cymbals of Astarte, and instead heard a mouse pulling my empty sardine-tin into the rocks. The labyrinths were full of life. Bats like dried-up shadows fidgeted in the fissures, and something invisible gargled and stamped a tiny, autocratic foot. In the morning a goatherd passed, playing a three-holed flute, and left the sounds behind him, haunting and Phrygian, in the temples.

I went east along the Roman road against the slopes of Kesrouan and Sannin. Here, as in the sculptured stones, nature mimicked man. Across the Nahr el Leban, the River of Milk, she had flung a bridge a hundred and fifty feet, so symmetrical that early archaeologists thought the Romans must have hewn it. But there was no sign of a chisel-stroke, no niche nor dedication to Caesar or the immortal gods; only the panic of the green river, and the arch, of heavy magnificence, from cliff to cliff.

Underneath, the water blew a cold wind and the hills had thrown down boulders so huge that I walked across them feeling the earth to be in spate. Its savagery was of nature only, virgin Astarte: the river cold and primal, poured out not for man but for itself. It promised that nature could go on, thrusting and insensible and building more enduringly than man, and here at the world's end had made a bridge, the most civilized structure of

[95]

all, which might last into eternity. Only the swifts lent a film of softness, twittering high up in the spray.

Later I reached the source of the River of Milk, which flowed from under ice, bursting its dam, and for three days I camped by a house which the snows had crumpled. The river is famous for its coldness, and clean winds blow up from the sea.

I circled the glen and turned west, following a new road through an empty village and seeing the whole Dog valley before me, russet and warm. Summer casinos have destroyed the beauty which they set out to exploit, and the Spring of Honey bursts from the hills. 'The waters of Milk and Honey', runs a local conceit, 'flow into the Dog's mouth.'

I stayed with a man named Messiah, who owned a bar. He had found a copy of *Gutes Wohnen,* and had decorated the place in the Tyrolean way as best he could, with ploughing harness, a pale-furred fox which he had shot on Sannin, and a pair of breach-loading *Ibrahimiye,* left behind by the Egyptians on their flight up the Dog River in 1841.

'What,' he asked, 'do you think of my bar?'

I admired it.

He switched on coloured lighting, which glowed behind whisky bottles and rams' horns. Another switch, and Circean music played.

We ate gluttonously. Occasionally people from the village would look in—old men in *cheroual,* who had heard the clink of arak glasses. They trod quickly and softly in and out, like Bunyan's Christian walking through the Valley of the Shadow of Death. One of them said that harnesses were for bullocks, not restaurants.

Only Messiah's mother stayed with us: a woman with dark-lidded, Slavic eyes. As each dish was consumed, she firmly stated its origin. 'Our cow,' she said as the *lebne* vanished. 'Our grapes,' when the arak gurgled. Messiah said that she did not like the bar, but wanted to be with him. His father would not come in; his business was to tend fruit trees. I only saw him once, when we met in the passage in the middle of the night. He looked at me greyly, then decided that I could not exist, and shuffled away.

Messiah's interests were ski-ing, hunting and women, but he had broken his leg and arm in a fall, and when he took his arak his hand quivered. So only women remained. The Greek girls, he said, were beautiful, and the French and Swiss and Italian; but he was not sure where all these countries were. If he made his way to Italy, he wondered, might he swoop down on Greece and Switzerland?

'Girls are my whole life. I even left school because I was mad with love. Do you suppose that if I got a boat to Paris . . .?'

But it would take two years to save money and reach Europe. He pulled a face, finished the arak and yawned. Reluctantly he switched off the loudspeaker, which carried jazz to the street outside, and slowly, one by one, the dogs in the village ceased to howl.

I awoke early, left Messiah and walked downriver past fields abandoned to wild orchids. The nineteenth-century missionary J. L. Porter, who rode all over the Middle East, called this the grandest country he had ever known. The Dog River is invisible, deep-carved in many-coloured stone. Beyond it the hills fade to the Barouk mountains, and the texture of the rocks against the haze, and the twisting of the river, lend depth and contrast at every point, like a well-planned garden.

The villages of the Kesrouan are mellow with tawny stone and slender-belfried churches: Hrajel, Meyrouba, Bekaata. And beyond the pink roofs of Achkout I saw Beirut, distinguishable from a low cloud only by the fingers of its harbour, put out greyly on a gold glass of sea. By the time I reached Reyfoun on the lip of the river it was dark, and I heard from a doorway a greeting which had grown familiar. Where was I going? Where would I sleep? It was dangerous outside. His home was mine. *Ahelan wasahelan!* Come. Come.

This was a young family, two brothers and a sister. Their father travelled in Iraq selling apples and their mother had died a few months before. One of the brothers had married. His wife was fair and plump and clung to his arm, butting her head against him; she was not beautiful, but dove-like and startled by happiness, the innocence unbroken which gives to first love a quality of childhood.

Her husband was a lorry-driver, who took soft limestone from the mountains to the cement kilns, where it was shovelled into water-tanks. He crumbled a piece in his hands and dropped it in a glass of water.

'Watch.'

For a while nothing happened. Then the rock began to shift and break up cloudily. We stared at it, the lorry-driver, his brother, sister and the fair-haired wife. And into the silence from the bottom of the glass came a low, anguished whine. Bubbles rose and burst through the thick paste and in a while the whole glassful was boiling and cracking and spilling over the table.

'That is what happens in the kilns,' said the lorry-driver.

His sister picked up the breaking glass and scolded him, conscious of her new authority as the lady of the house. She was beautiful, with soft, animated features; and instead of the mountain sturdiness she was willowy as a Botticelli Grace. Khalil, her younger brother, said that she had made it her duty to smile with them ever since her mother's death. Recently she had returned from Jerusalem where she had walked the stations of the Via Dolorosa and prayed for her mother at the Holy Sepulchre; and when she was quiet and the mobility left her face, it was adult and sad.

Once she had been engaged, but her father had thought the man unsuitable and sent him away. I asked Khalil if she had loved him, but he did not know. He had not thought of asking. His thoughts were always with his mother.

'She never went out of the house. Her care was always for us. She worked from before dawn. She never stopped.' In the morning when we walked in the village, people still offered their condolences. A woman was working in her garden, and looking up to see us cried, 'Why do I always work here? What is the use? *Ma baka fiyi!* Your mother always worked in her garden just like me. Where did it take her? After all her work, where is she?'

Sometimes the questions were spat out in a set inquisition and had to be answered according to custom. And Khalil always murmured thanks. He was unmoved. He may have found personalism and tenderness in the cries, but to me they were spent in helpless ritual, the people entering into grief as into something changeless and familiar, wailing for themselves too, for toil and meaninglessness, for all the dead and all the living.

'When my sister marries I shall be alone,' said Khalil, looking bovine and miserable. 'I shall have to marry too. I loved a girl for four years. Then one day she disappeared. Her parents had married her to somebody else.'

He had loved her at sixteen, when ideals and passion were blended. Now he confessed to lust, not for her only but for women in general, and he thought that the satisfaction of his body might cancel the loss in his mind. But the body goes on wanting and is easily acquitted, as he was discovering in Beirut. The trouble was in the heart, which no longer believed, but remained in suspension, waiting for a sign. So the body was degraded where it might have been transformed.

Our truest emotions are selfish, wrote Stendhal. From the animal the ideal draws strength in love and is complete: flame from ember, word from flesh, Aphrodite from Astarte.

Qalat Fakra: altar and tower

Qalat Fakra: sculpture of nature

Bridge of Ice

Bridge of Stone

10. The Dog River

> . . . here up the gleaming forest glades,
> By Lebanon's romantic arms embraced,
> Gay Pleasure's votaries mixed in dance, in song;
> And built their breathing bowers on Thammuz' side
> . . . Love, in his prime
> A rosy infant.
>
> Anon: *Lebanon*, 1819

THE DOG RIVER, valley of depth and stillness. Often it seems that no river runs there, so steep and close are the spurs along its course, as if they brushed together as they fell. The mountaineers chose its crags for monasteries, eyried and battered like Rhenish castles: Louaiza, site of the Maronite union with Rome; Christ-Roi, Mar Abda and Antoura, where Burckhardt and Lamartine stayed. Not even a goat track descends to the river. I climbed down for hundreds of feet, sliding among stones, hearing them fall far below awaking the valley's loneliness; rested by wild lilies, sensing the mounting of the round-headed pines up the hill and their Mediterranean fragrance, heavy with summer nights; and at last saw the river, more corridor than valley, but bright and flexuous, like a reptile.

The Greeks called the river Lycus, 'the Wolf', but ancient geographers, who knew little of Lebanon, do not tell why. In later myth some god or demon chained to the river's mouth a monstrous wolf, and when it was lashed by the waves, its bellows could be heard in Cyprus. But others said that on stormy days the sea cried like a beast in the hollows of the promontory and from this arose the legend and the name.

Yet a white plinth stands on a headland at the valley's mouth above the sea, and an Arab tradition tells that the statue of a wolf stood here and barked a warning when an enemy fleet appeared upon the skyline. Perhaps this was a carving of the jackal-god Anubis, for the country was steeped in the cults of Egypt. The body of Osiris was washed up on the nearby shores and Isis, when she came to find him, was aided by Anubis.

In a high wind the statue was said to moan, as did a Colossus of Memnon, and the Arabs, who feared these sounds, heaved the strange animal into the waves. Dr Pococke, early in the eighteenth century, saw a stone sunken in the sea beneath the cliff where the pedestal stood and was told that this was the wolf. And in 1942, during the construction of the railway beneath the point, Australian sappers unearthed a statue, wave-worn but recognizable, of a dog or wolf.

The river flows among boulders and maples. The scented woods reminded me of walks by other rivers, but all nameless, as if years of leaves and mornings were present there. I saw an Arab bridge, graceful and old, a single arch across the river; here the glen widened to a valley of lemon trees beneath an aqueduct, and the road to Faraya passed, and in the gorge arose the Christ-Roi monastery on whose summit a fifty-foot Saviour opened His arms to the sea.

Near the river's mouth is a stepped and cobbled bridge built by the Mameluke sultan Barkuk and restored by Emir Bechir with three mellow arches of unequal size. And on the north bank an aqueduct of unknown age runs high along the cliff, cut into the rock or carried on stilted arches, fountained in vines. Where the river meets the sea it is crossed by the modern road and railway, and the Turks built a low bridge which is still used.

Before these passageways were cut, the headland fell sheer into the waves. It was the obstacle and bulwark of the Phoenician coast, and catalyst of many battles. Baldwin of Boulogne, with only a hundred and sixty knights of the First Crusade, faced a Damascene army here and was cut off to the north by a squadron of Arab ships. But he feigned a dawn retreat and drew the Syrians on, then turned and routed them and crossed the Dog next morning, unopposed.

The ancient Egyptians hacked a road which wound across the southern cliff in steps, and the Romans followed them, traversing the point more boldly at its crown. Proud with their conquests, successive empires carved tokens on the rock, and with an odd reverence left each other's monuments as they were cut.

In 587 B.C., while his army besieged Jerusalem, Nebuchadnezzar II carved a memorial on the Lycus and in the forest of Hermel. The letters are neat and oddly small, chipped in columns on the north bank of the river in the old and new cuneiform of Babylon. Water has seeped greenly from the aqueduct above and furrowed away many words, but from the Hermel carvings the gaps in the text are filled. With an ageless imperialistic cunning the king declares that an enemy is looting and depopulating Lebanon and that he has taken it upon himself to restore its people to happiness.

'What no former king had done, I achieved: I cut through steep mountains, I split rocks, opened passages and constructed a straight road for the transportation of the cedars. I made the Ahratu float down and carry to Marduk, my king, mighty cedars, high and strong, of precious beauty and of excellent dark quality, the abundant yield of the Lebanon, as if they be reed stalks carried by the river . . . I made the inhabitants of the Lebanon live in safety together and let nobody disturb them. In order that nobody might do any harm to them I erected there a statue showing me as everlasting king of the region. . . .'

But it was not until fourteen years later that the hostile Egyptians were defeated and Ethobaal II, stubborn king of Tyre, replaced by a puppet prince. The real foe was rebellious Judah. A year after a Chaldean mason had chipped the king's inscription on the Dog River, Jerusalem fell and the Temple was destroyed, and King Zedekiah's sons were killed in front of him before he was blinded. The children of Israel went into their long captivity in Babylon, and nothing more was carved on the Lycus until the Romans came.

Walking to the headland, I saw on the southern bank the memorial of Sultan Barkuk, who records the construction of his bridge in a faded, fluorescent script, as if the waters had flowed over it. And a quarter of a mile beyond, an inscription was raised to commemorate the widening of the Roman road over the headland during the principate of the emperor Caracalla; 'he widened the road to the Lycus River by high mountains . . .'; but the name of the Third Legion Gallica, which undertook the work but mutinied a few years later, was erased from the plaque.

Above it a tablet records the Allied capture of Damascus in 1941, and a cenotaph has been raised to the French army and navy, 'Liberators of Syria and Lebanon'. Next door, in contradiction, is General Gouraud's commemoration of his capture of Damascus from the Syrians in 1920, chalked with signs of local disapproval. And Napoleon III, with his usual boorishness, erased an ancient Egyptian inscription to carve the legend of his 1860 campaign.

It is not known when the Egyptians first built a road over the promontory, but the Phoenicians and Romans followed the first part of their route, and Assyrian kings set sculptures of themselves below. The road climbs south beneath an inscription of

Tatianus Proclus, Byzantine governor in Heliopolis. Even here the point dominates the shore. The mountains become insubstantial and the sea calm. The Egyptian way ascends the hill steeply where wild hollyhocks grow; the Roman drives across the promontory and ends in mid-air as the modern tunnel cuts it away. Where the roads part there stands the pedestal of white carved stone from which the wolf-dog may have gazed to sea. The older stairway winds up by the carvings of Assyrian and Egyptian, side by side. The Assyrian stands in prayer or sacrifice and is well-preserved, even to the wrinkles of his beard and the ridge of his wand. Herodotus said that Ramses II had covered the eastern Mediterranean with his memorials, and the Egyptian sculpture is his, carved while he warred against the Hittites thirty-two centuries ago. The wind has picked out the long inscription but left it decipherable, and the stick-like figures of god and pharaoh are still arrogant in the stone.

On the headland's crown a third Assyrian king, better preserved, postures in the same sacrifice; and the last pair of carvings lie below, more exposed than any to the sea. Viewed from in front the Egyptian stele is meaningless, mere dribblings in the cliff, but seen a few feet to east or west the figures awaken from the rock: the god Ammon stands with his tall crown, and Ramses raises his arm to strike a prisoner thrown before him.

Beside them, like a finished pattern born of many models, is the best-preserved Assyrian king. He is stern and handsome as the other kings were once, with firm nose and pursed lips, curled locks and the spired crown. A wolf on the fold. In his right hand he holds a cedar bough and with his left arm cradles the sovereign mace. And a herb has grown out from the rock and presses a bouquet to the cruel fist. Around him and across his robes, seeming delicate and incidental as an insect's scratchings, run lines of cuneiform. The king, they say, was Esarhaddon, who in 671 B.C. invaded Egypt, slew her vassal rulers in Phoenicia and pursued the prince of Tyre, who fled to Cyprus, and 'fished him like a fish out of the sea, brought him back, and cut off his head.'

Yet the Assyrians, the great destroyers, set their own carvings beside those of Egypt on the headland, and did not think to blemish or obliterate. They may have recognized the vulnerability of their own names, or the brotherhood of their gods; but neither Persians, Greeks nor iconoclast Moslems touched the inscriptions. Perhaps the majesty of the headland deterred them, or the awesome passage of time, or the hieratic grandeur of the god-kings themselves, mounting their early roadway to the sky.

*   *   *

The holiness which men attached to rivers was never greater than in Lebanon. Springing from cisterns in the mountains, scooped out of limestone by the winter rain, they flowed through valleys of such steepness that their directions seemed meaningful and settled for ever. These galleries of caves, and the ancient sureness that the world was flat, lent a special strangeness to the waters, grown from the mystery of earth and merging with the sky. Even now, when a new spring erupts from the mountains, the country people assemble as if at a place of miracle, and hope to heal their sickness in its virginity.

Only four miles from its mouth, the Dog River finds its most abundant source in the caves beneath Jeita village. They were first explored in 1873, by two engineers from the Water Company of Beirut. They took a raft of inflated goatskins, and lighting their way with manganese wires, found themselves floating on an underground river. For ten hours they followed it into the mountain, reaching no end, and placed a record of their expedition in a bottle, setting it on a stalagmite where the lime-filled water has fixed and covered it. Many explorers came after them, dragging their boats up the rapids, and penetrated the mountain for four miles; but they too found no end.

Now the rock formations have been illumined and the current diverted, so that for half a mile the water lies unruffled in the hill. As the caves are entered the river sounds secret and rebellious below. A barge rides on a pool. Here the steersman waits a while for visitors, then pushes away where the rock-face bends low.

The boat passes beneath a black arch as through a picture-frame, floating down an avenue of stillness under the cold-lit rocks. These seem crystalline, delicate, leaving no cliff-face bare, as if their richness was the natural state of stone. Often one cannot know how high the mute cascades are falling, out of such clefts of darkness do they come, and as they pour against the water their reflections lift themselves through the deep and touch with their points the limits of its shadow.

The guide remains bored and speechless at the prow of the boat, working his paddle, and does not point out organ-pipes or spires or faces misshapen in the rock. So one moves in silence through the womb of earth, finding it not virgin, but of unsounded depth and a kind of grief-stricken beauty. It is hard to remember that this has been made only by rain seeping into Cretaceous limestone, leaving shades of ochre, fawn and salmon patternless. Yet every cavern is moved by a subtle life, seeming frozen but never still, the water dripping forever into the hushed rocks. The boat enters them as into rooms, passing by passageways where it scrapes against the cliffs. The stalactites appear to shuffle and wave, and sometimes glint with sequin lights. And all these halls, miasmic, almost vegetable, seem to await a tenant, some hoary spelaean king, his limbs grown crusted and stalactic, his wand an icicle, rowed on a mollusc wherry by a crew of trolls.

But the halls pass on, superb and empty, cathedral beauty to no god, and the boatman thrusts his paddle to the rock, and turns around and steers back to the light.

*   *   *

'I am an Assyrian,' said the doorkeeper of the Sarba monastery.

Most history books announced the decease of the Assyrians twenty-six centuries ago. I thought of them, like Sumerians, as chapters and illustrations. So I looked at him foolishly, as if expecting him to sprout a plaited beard, and asked him where his people lived.

'Iraq, naturally. I come from Baghdad.'

What was he doing in Lebanon?

'I was shot in the leg and the government gave me compensation, so I came here.'

'How were you shot?'

'Fighting.'

Of course. An Assyrian. 'Are there many of your people left?'

'Yes, many. We are a great people. There are ninety thousand of us. And here is another. He is the monastery chauffeur.' The other man shook my hand. They looked the same, like the Dog River kings. They were agile and soldierly, well-knit, with narrow heads; but one was a porter and the other a chauffeur. I felt as if I had seen Sennacherib at the gates of Jerusalem, begging.

'Life is better in Lebanon than with us. We have finished with Iraq now. We will stay here. You know how much I can earn . . .?'

I was thinking of the great nation of Assyria standing in his face, the Sargons and Tiglath-Pilesers, exactors of tribute and movers of tribes.

'. . . I couldn't find a job in Iraq which would pay me half as well.'

Had they seen Nineveh?

Yes, they said. They pronounced it *Nine-eh-wah*. Only stones.

And Ashur?

Ashoor. More stones.

The Assyrians were almost extinguished by the Medes and Babylonians in 610 B.C. and afterwards existed as a small community, atoning in many persecutions for the cruelty with which they had reigned. Now they lived in Baghdad, or were barbers in San Francisco or chauffeurs in Lebanon. It was absurd to be surprised.

Priests came out of the chapel for Corpus Christi and ambled in procession through the cloisters. The Assyrians crossed themselves. There was an old woman, bent double, in black fur slippers, who could not follow the procession, but sat in the garden, looking at the trees and smiling to herself.

The Sarba monastery was built ninety years ago by Greek Catholic monks from Aleppo. They bought a site three miles north of the Dog River and placed their foundation on an ancient acropolis overlooking the pure, deep curve of Jounie bay. The cloisters are lightly made, carried on pointed Arabic arches and enclosing a garden. But in the base of the northern walls lie cyclopean stones from the early temple, ranged in five courses and greyed from the wind. Over one doorway is carved a lost eastern deity, and in an aperture of the wall stands a bull-headed console. It is perhaps a carving of Serapis, a fusion of Osiris and the bull-god Apis, an Egyptian mongrel, and it took its place easily in the monastery among the Roman walls, the Assyrians, and the priests in white, Byzantine pageant through the garden.

Sarba was the acropolis for the town of Palaeobyblos, whose port may have been Jounie. It lay on the road which the Romans paved along the coast, and a few of its stones are still lodged in the houses on the hill. Beneath the monastic kitchens a passage runs to the sea underground. Railroad workers blundered into it while cutting round the point and blocked it up, but it was seen to lead to a grotto by the shore, called the Cave of St George.

Sarba grew pretty and intimate as I descended, imagining the line of the tunnel below, and passing the garden 'Tomb of the Princess' down balustraded stairs and honeyed cliffs. Below the monastery, rocks lay in the water where the cave was broken by the sea. The waves had washed it clean and left a pool, and beneath the concave rock a gallery of green reflections spread, and lost itself in darkness.

Niches had been hollowed from the cliff in early times and steps cut steeply to the water. The largest niche was black with smoke and white with candle-grease, and supplicants had stuck coins and pebbles there. The scarp above was hewn out in antiquity, when the cave was larger, the holes still open where the beams were jointed in. And from a placard St George, armoured as a Gothic knight, stood out in bas-relief and slew his dragon. St George, the Green One: Adonis reincarnate. He haunts all the countryside of Byblos. This known association of the saint and god, and the grotto carved anciently and linked to the Sarba temple underground, tell that the waters here were sacred to Adonis.

As I stepped down to the pool I heard a baby crying in the hollow rocks, and looking over the ledge I saw a man hold his naked child above the stagnant water. Across its pudgy body curled a rash, and its mouth was frothing. Its mother stood before the votive niche and held up another child, so it might fix a coin against the blackened wall. Here St George gives health for children. The pool is soft and shy with light, quiet in three thousand years of holiness. When the child is dipped below the surface, the god is there unseen in the green water, touching, healing.

Out at sea a liner was sailing to Beirut, and cranes and motor-yachts stood in the flat jetties of Jounie.

'Dip him,' said the mother.

Gently the father dropped his infant to the filmy pool. The insects moved away in rippling lights, and the child, now quiet, alighted on the waters of Adonis.

11. The Anger of Artemis

> Adonis, while hunting, was killed
> by a boar through the anger of Ar-
> temis.
>
> *Apollodorus*

THE QUEST has been a walk in darkness with open eyes. The goddess has kept her essence unknown, for the things which men know they rob of their divinity. But her progress through time, and the changes wrought in her, have been sensed here and there where she covered her traces lightly: the high places and sacred waters, the veiling presence of the Holy Virgin, of St George, the mystery of ruined towers, altars under cedar groves, and the changeless witness of the night sky.

There was a time, of course, when men were faithful and she showed herself more clearly. But the testimony of those centuries, broken along the Phoenician shore, is like a temple ruin in which only random columns point the lines the building may have followed. Faintly the emergence of Astarte in faith may be detected, and how as Aphrodite, made beautiful in the statuary and pastorals of Europe, she lost her meaning and died a slow death through the years of Greece and Rome.

But in Lebanon itself her powers were vital to the end and she faded into the Christian morn still holy. So for a moment, before descending to Byblos and Adonis country, I probed at a special point in time: those years when the goddess could last be recognized, standing in a blaze of worship before the Roman sun went down.

Under the Hellenic kings who ruled after Alexander, the art and science of the classical world dominated the Phoenician shore. Baths and theatres crowded its cities, and the wealthy took to Greek clothes and language, and began to feel a sense of individual dignity and a love of life for its own sake. So when Pompey came in 64 B.C. and gave *Provincia Syria* to the Empire, he found a coast of rich and ancient towns, which to a superficial eye were Hellenized.

The Romans consolidated the Greek beginnings, bringing order and security, and stretched their highways from well-built harbours, linking their colonnaded cities with the world. But beneath the European skin still beat a Semitic heart. The Canaanite language died, but the tongue which replaced it was Aramaic. The country people lived forgotten as they had always done, and in the temples of Haddad, Eshmun and Astarte the old divinities took new names but kept their attributes. To the end of the Seleucid era the Phoenician kings still bore the titles of their gods, and were high priests in Sidon. The classical pantheon proved weaker than the Semitic. It became orientalized. Jupiter and Haddad were confounded together as fathers of the sky, but the mode of worship was eastern, and Astarte and Adonis suffered little change.

After two and a half centuries of Roman rule, inland Phoenicia, grown populous, became part of the new province called Hollow Syria. Many new towns prospered in the vale of the Beqaa, where Baalbec stands, and here, withdrawn in the mountains, the Roman cities outlived the Roman Empire and left their golden frames among the fields.

The valley is carved with tenderness and grandeur, cupped in a long stadium of hills which reach imperceptibly to snow. It was almost June when I camped under poplars in the eastern valley at Anjar, ancient Chalcis. Here once the road from Heliopolis, today's Baalbec, went south to Sidon and was crossed by eastern caravans as they journeyed from Damascus to the sea. Strabo said that when the Romans came, Chalcis was the capital of Ptolemy, the son of Mennaeus. His country stretched from Heliopolis, already a great shrine, for more than sixty miles southward to the lava fields of Trachonitis, strangling Damascus; and his people were Ituraean brigands. But he was executed by Mark Antony for helping the Parthians, and Chalcis passed as a gift of love to Cleopatra, who delegated it to Zenodorus. But his was a robber-kingdom for which the Roman Empire had no place, and after 22 B.C. the city's territories were given to neighbouring provinces until it commanded little more than the land which could be seen from its rooftops.

The sadness of Chalcis lay under a snow of thistledown, its blond stones overgrown or scattered orderless among the trees. I could see the weeds rising from a cistern's bed, and the fish between them smeared with light, and the upthrust of old stones. Its feel is now of softness and oblivion, the waters dribbling to a river spread with Monet lilies; stones and water, and man's need for them, at rest under the slanting shade.

Augustus took the princedom when Zenodorus died, and

granted it to Herod the Great, for it was hard to rule; and years later the Emperor Claudius gave it to the brother of Herod Agrippa with the title of king. He governed it until his death, with his queen Berenice, who afterwards became her own brother's mistress, until Titus came to Syria to fight against the Jews and fell in love with her, and made her his consort in Rome.

It was Herod Agrippa's brother who built a temple to the south of Chalcis on the hill called Mejdel Anjar. But long before him the Ptolemies had held a fortress here, which Antiochus the Great besieged, and which for two hundred years guarded the pastoral city of the brigand-kings.

The porticoes of Herod's temple have fallen from it, but the cella rises sheer, its stones so eroded that they have grown together jointless and the wind has shaved them raw and veined as a flayed body. The temple was turned into a castle again long after classical times, the great red pillars laid for foundations and the shrine turned to a keep, where fluted semi-columns have faded in the walls.

So the memory of Herod vanished, as the running of wind over stone. The Romans gave his son a better kingdom, called Chalcis too, where his reign was long and prosperous, and his queen was Salome, who had danced as a girl before Herod Antipas and asked as her reward the head of John the Baptist.

Six hundred years later the remains of Chalcis were found by Walid I, caliph in Damascus and ruler of half the world. He had them assembled where they had fallen, by the green springs of Anjar, and built a pleasure-city ringed with walls of dressed stone and forty towers hung close together. And the lineaments of the town are still enclosed there, almost a mile in circuit, giving access by towered gates to straight classical ways.

I entered with the guiltiness of an intruder, looking back up each trespassed street, surprised at my solitude. The buildings stood familiarly in variegated brick and stone, the lines of the porticoes drawn by truncated pillars, and the courts held lonely columns.

The Damascus caliphs were desert men by instinct, free in thought and body, who ruled irreverently before Mahomet's memory was faint. Often when summer stifled Damascus they rode to the cooling winds of Anjar. Bangled salukis yawned on villa steps, and wine and dancing made the nights corrupt where the palace still rises between the mountains, as if within a shining outer wall.

From the Roman strength of Anjar the Arabs plucked

refinement. Delicately they carved the heavy blocks, rebuilt the streets which met at tetrapylons, and raised a city vivid and eccentric, filled with aesthetic heresies against the classical world. They shaped their statues with ebullience, like the sculpture of Hauran, with the same artificial ribbing of the robes, and the skirts belling out. And over every arch and lintel the Islamic carving spread, fastidious and pale, turning the stone to flowers.

But this borrowed grandeur evokes nothing serious, only a vague distaste or amusement, as if children had made their den in a ruined mansion. Nearby were more meaningful signs: shacks like card-houses which crowded the ruins. Thick, hirsute men stood in their doorways and extended their hands solemnly to me and asked if there was anything I needed. But behind this courtesy they were awaiting something. Their eyes were not hostile, but curious. They were expecting war. In their hands they held their little transistor radios, in which Radio Cairo crackled and declaimed: 'We will drive the Israelis into the sea. . . .' For two weeks the Egyptians had been mobilized against Israel in Gaza and Sinai, the Jordanians and Syrians in the east, Lebanon to the north. The United Nations forces had been withdrawn. Everybody knew that war would break out at some time. The Palestinians were poised, half anxious, half exuberant.

On the village outskirts stood a boy with a goat. I asked him what was happening.

'War,' he piped, grinning. 'Very soon.' With his twig-like arms and distended stomach, he looked like a famine-relief poster. 'We will drive the Israelis into the sea.'

I slept poorly and at dawn wandered along the river, brushing away blackthorn from the tired stones of Chalcis; then northward through the arcaded streets of Qabb Elias, where donkeys walked meekly at the head of camel-trains, like dwarfs leading kings.

Above the town was the last wall of a Druse castle, rubble almost, its windows worn to Gothic filaments. Later, soldiers went by in lorries to Israel. They were singing. A band of nomads was trailing down the road too. They seemed to go with the same sense of purpose as the soldiers, the women handsome under their stiff black headdress, the half-moons gleaming in their noses, driving their flocks and children to the west.

As the last lorry passed, they flowed over the road, and five truck-drawn gun-carriages, which were following the infantry, became enmeshed among camels. The soldiers hooted and blasphemed and roared the engines, but the camels, looking starchy and faintly affronted, spread across the road in arrowhead formation and continued shambling toward some distant pasture. The trucks tried to sneak around their flanks, but the camels deployed and regrouped with derisive roars, while the nomad women yelled and beat them helplessly, their sticks thumping and breaking on the hairless flanks. The infantry trucks had long since vanished over the hills, unaware that they had been deprived of their artillery.

The camels were not being purposely obstructionist, but were supra-national camels, asserting only the need to move from pasture to pasture, not from peace to war. Frontiers have never concerned the nomads. They see only waste and fertile spaces, with towns between, and their view is less artificial than ours. So the great padded camel feet rose and fell pacifistically, and when last I saw the nomads, they were trailing down the road in a stream of assertive cheerfulness, the sounds of hooting drowned in contralto camel bells.

It was the time of year when the dwarf oaks drop the spiny casings of their fruit, as if baby hedgehogs had shed their skins. I settled in their shadow and watched a nomad woman with a child in her arms come walking over the plain. She squatted in front of me and cast a handful of shells into the dust.

'Your mother wishes you to go one way; you have gone another,' she said, studying the fall of the shells. This was very likely; my mother would be wanting me out of the country because of the impending war. The woman, by her dress, came from the Syrian desert and she had black unethereal eyes which did not look as if they could see anything but the immediate present.

'You have brothers who are far from you,' she said.

That was a poor guess. I had no brothers. I relaxed.

'You are in danger.' That was easy too; there was a war coming.

The pearly shells clinked in the dust again.

'There is a woman you love but will not marry.'

I paid attention.

'You will be going a long way now. The mountains, the sea. When you finish you will be happy. You are going to Baalbec. Give me twenty piastres.'

The gold in her child's hair flashed as she walked away.

[113]

Signs were beginning to appear in the hills. At Qabb Elias some early Semitic people had hacked an altar or a monument out of the fevered cliffs, facing the rising sun. And on the hills near Fourzol a rock-cut sanctuary bore the carving of a cone, a phallic emblem perhaps; while in a niche a sculptured horseman plucked some fruit and a man before him held a bunch of grapes. It is not known who carved these shrines: Arameans, perhaps, in honour of Haddad and Atargatis, or the Nabateans of Petra who came northward in the century before Christ and sanctified high places to Dushara. For the sculptures depict life again, extroverted, humble, emphatic; eyes turned out to God, not into man.

The valley is old to religion. Out of pre-classical times a legend grew that here the Great Flood first ran dry. The ark of Noah alighted not on Mount Ararat but on Sannin, and Noah stepped from it, seeing the first rainbow spring from Anjar, and grazed his flocks along the fertile plain. With one stride he could cross the valley, and the sepulchre which he built for himself was cast from a mountain. But God grew angry with him before he died, and destroyed it, so he was buried in a slender tomb in the village of Kerak, where Christians and Moslems pray to him.

Kerak has been swallowed by Christian Zahlé, which has a name for insolence, but the sepulchre lies obscure behind gardens, joined to a Mameluke mosque. The caretaker opens the door with reverence and exposes the tomb: a ridge of dressed stone nearly a hundred and five feet long, covered with silks and partly a Roman aqueduct.

The villagers of Kerak are divided about it on minor issues. Noah, say some, had to be folded up like a paper doll before he would fit into the grave. Others are certain that only his torso was buried, and that God smashed the rest. The Noah of the Koran is self-righteous, while in the Bible he appears gentle, enjoyed wine and lived to a marvellous age. But Christians and Moslems are happy in their mutual shrine and are not surprised at its length, for 'There were giants in the earth in those days, mighty men, who were of old, men of renown.' They groaned under lake waters and lived among the crags around Moab and Bashan; and as late as the eleventh century B.C. Jonathan slew 'a man of great stature, that had on every hand six fingers, and on every foot six toes, four and twenty in number; and he also was born to the giant.'

Like most giants they appear to have been stupid and melancholy, and to have faded away before history found them.

Their cyclopean tombs are scattered through the anti-Lebanon: Abel above the Barada valley; Nimrod on Hermon; Seth, the third son of Adam, at Nebi Shiit. The fossils of diluvian animals may have inspired their myths, or the deep cave-tombs of early men, or the Chalcolithic dolmens of Jordan and the Syrian hills. And like children who love the miraculous, Semitic tribes have passed down a history transformed with ogres and the heroes who slew them.

The Romans left ruins all through the central valley, and the villagers, of course, have reused them. Mostly these must have been humdrum towns, seated comfortably on the trade highway south from Heliopolis: Ksarnaba, the vanished shrine of 'The Monastery of the Gazelle', and the sunken temple of Jdita, dedicated on a broken altar-side to Juno, for the health of Antoninus Pius; all fallen when Byzantium withdrew and the old trade flowed in other channels, or ceased to flow at all.

So in many villages one may walk through modern streets and see suddenly, set careless in a wall, the inscribed certainty of another time: '. . . this to Jupiter . . .'

The ancient historians are silent on these cities, even on Niha, whose temples were rich. Niha valley is an intimate and watered slit in Sannin's eastern foothills. The temples rise secluded and grand in its mildness, and a stream flows between. On one side is a nameless shrine whose steps are white and faultless where the hillside broke down and protected them, scattering Ionic columns. Beside it fell the fragment of an entablature, so preserved in the dark earth that its chiselled lion's head is complete and ready, with the paint still ochreous in its eyes and jaws. Disquieting perfection. And in the temple opposite, among the stones which two millennia had made their own, a chance slip of earth had kept a cornice sunless almost from its shaping, until the excavators pulled it into time.

The temple is a blending of two ways: eastern faith blazes in the Roman order. It was dedicated to Hadaranis, an obscure Syrian god, and was served by sacred virgins or prostitutes. The Romans cut a road above, leading from orchards to a barren upland, and paved it with rounded stones, polished as marble now, and hacked through sheer rock at the valley's crest. The blue and grey of evening soothed all nakedness. Even the pebbled hills withdrew their edges, twilight falling, and returning farmers were shadows riding on the soft pelt of the dark.

A temple is cradled in the hills beside a stream, and as the Niha sanctuary shares its valley's richness and humanity, so this shrine, looking on rocks, seems to have taken their strength and plainness to itself. Inside its cella the iron-grey stones cascade. They are carved poor and shallow, with no surprise of lions beneath the earth, for the wind has pummelled the masks into expressions of the stone itself. And I could not discover what divinity was worshipped there.

I walked down the valley again through dusk and the tinkling of unseen goats. No limpid eastern twilight. A man had planted rose-bushes for scent along the stream, and was picking the flowers. He looked up as I went by, and gathering his evening's labour in an apron, came over to me and poured it into my arms. I accepted two roses, hung them behind my ears and walked down to Niha, feeling light. In Sinai Egyptian troops were crowding towards Israel, 'the puppet of the West'. The Sixth Fleet cruised beyond Cyprus, and Russian ships were passing south to the Bosporus. But in this small valley, with a look of privilege and a gesture of simplicity, an Arab villager had handed me his roses. I wore them like a banner down the Roman road.

The village priest found me making camp beneath the temple of Hadaranis and asked me to his house. We sat out on a patio by lamplight with his family. But soon the radio ceased to play music and began broadcasting against the West. The voice was angry and authoritative. Nobody wished to call attention to it by turning it off. It sat amongst us like a person, while we judged it and tried to come to an agreement over what it was saying, while talking of other things. Finally the priest switched it off with his foot.

'It is time for bed,' he said.

His bedroom was furnished only by a gun and a wooden cross sealed for preservation in a bottle of water. He stood in the red glow of a night-bulb, and prayed; and long after the room was in darkness I could hear his mumbling and the faint scratching of his fingers on his cardigan as he crossed himself.

I fell asleep before he had finished and awoke at dawn, thinking for a moment that I lay under the temple of Hadaranis. Then I turned to see the priest's elliptical shape in the bed opposite, his beard gushing over the blankets, his stomach rising in a friendly mound. He stirred too, and twiddled his toes, which stuck out beyond the end of the bed, and decided he must be awake. Quickly he traced a cross and launched into prayer,

Mount Sannin

Maronite hillsman

Greek Catholic farmer

The Dog River

but after a while he said quietly to God, or to himself, 'Enough!' and swung his feet to earth and called for coffee.

*   *   *

What the Hellenistic age lost in nobility, it may have gained in the humanity of its more complex time. But with the impotence of science and reason to find new assurances, a hollowness appeared in the later Greek world, the divided realms of Alexander, which was unknown to Periclean Athens. Pride and faith in the destiny of the city-state had been replaced by more subtle, introspective concerns. The old answers no longer satisfied. The Olympian gods went dumb.

Into this spiritual void, deepened by civil wars and strife with Rome, crept the mysteries and magic of the East. Superstition had not at any time been quiet, but now the promise extended by Osiris and Adonis, by Cybele and a crowd of minor cults, began to undermine the frigid systems of the Stoic, the Epicurean and the Cynic. In Greece itself the rites of Dionysus thrived, and hope came again in instinct and subservience: the watchwords of the East.

From such Semitic faith dressed up in classical beauty, Baalbec rose. The Arabs, reverent before its size, say that it was thrown up by Cain against the wrath of God or that Solomon, corrupted by his foreign wives, gave his heart to Astarte and built Baalbec in her name. The ancients are silent about its origins, as if it had always existed, and the name, probably meaning 'Lord of the Beqaa', betrays an archaic past. The Greek Seleucid kings called it Heliopolis, 'City of the Sun', and may have raised shrines here, though nothing is left of them. So the Romans built their temples on holy ground, probably beginning early in the first century A.D. and nearing completion two hundred years later in the reign of Septimius Severus, who minted coins portraying the Temple of Jupiter.

The whole temple-complex is raised on a cushion of stones. From it one may trace the sidling of the green Orontes before it sheds into Syria past ruined Apamea and Antioch, the bowels of the Seleucid empire, and to the south the Litani river gathers strength, and Hermon shows a white shoulder.

The entrance propylea, whose towers were turned to fortresses, spreads brokenly across the monumental steps. The pilasters of the towers are stripped away, but the pediments hang on the walls, and cockleshell niches are scooped out in them unharmed.

For a moment I thought I was walking through a pure Augustan splendour. But beyond the triple entrance spreads a hexagonal forecourt—unheard of in Rome—once intimate with porticoes and the stance of marble gods. There is a cult-stone of Jupiter-Haddad, flanked by bulls, his figure worn but his identity sure, crowned in the fanned-out calathos, his arms exclamatory around his body, quartered with faces of the lesser gods.

Beyond him, in the Court of Sacrifice, the majesty of Baalbec spreads like an autumn forest. Its dimensions alone would have bent a primitive mind to reverence, and one imagines that no temples in the world can testify to Roman ingenuity like these, and that none were laid out better or have so preserved the detail of their riches.

The portico is in fragments round the court, and the walls are deepened by pillared vestibules. Above attached columns the pedimented niches rise in double tiers and must have harboured a strange pantheon, the grace of Olympus married to the stiff, rude gods of Syro-Phoenicia. The stone is weathered to a look of frailty, but here and there the Corinthian architraves have been set up, showing a rich, Seleucid beauty, and beyond them the six columns of Jupiter rise like a blast of trumpets.

A centurion, in fulfilment of a vow, embossed with gold two capitals of the rose granite columns in the propylea, now gone, and carved a prayer for the Emperor Caracalla, and for his mother, Julia Domna. 'To the great Heliopolitan Jupiter, to Venus and Mercury, gods of Heliopolis . . .' But which of the temples each god inhabited is unknown. Perhaps, worshipped in trinity, their official and occult aspects were separately enshrined; but probably 'the great Heliopolitan Jupiter' owned the high temple, and his consort Astarte, who descended through Aphrodite to the Venus of the Romans, stood in the sanctuary below him.

The gods of earth and emotion are all about it. Its flower-motifs are eastern in their ebullience, and the running vines are Syrian which thread Astarte's gateway. The long basins in the Sacrificial Court were known to Phoenician temples, where Astarte's fish were kept; sculptured dragons spit and fly along their rims and there is a scramble of many non-existent beasts and faded sea-people holding wands and veils. Even Jupiter's sleek columns, sixty-five feet high, unfold into life at their tips, the acanthus leaves lifting an entablature of eggs and flowers, abundant as a Lebanese spring. Of fifty-four columns which sheathed his temple, a little larger than the Parthenon, these six only are upright. Justinian took eight and stood them in the apses of Haghia Sophia, and from others the Arabs bored out the lead joints for use in war, and earthquakes crippled them. The god's statue vanished when Rome became Christian, but early in the fifth century Macrobius described it as 'of gold, representing a person without a beard, who holds in his right hand a whip, charioteer-like, and in his left a thunderbolt together with ears of corn, all of which mark the united forms of Jupiter and the Sun'.

Sometimes the effigies of the divinities were washed in pools, and during processions would urge their bearers on supernaturally. To Jupiter blood-sacrifice was made in silence by the great hierophant in purple robes and crown of gold, while an army of white-clad priests stood watching.

There was here a famous oracle which foretold death to the emperor Trajan, but where it was housed is not known. In the Court of Sacrifice, beside the altar, are the foundations of a tower. It bears the trace of inside stairways and rose directly before the Temple of Jupiter, and in design, as far as one may tell, it resembles the tower at Qalat Fakra, built as a soft confusion for the mind.* Archaeologists, perplexed, have reconstructed it on paper and believe it to have contained four stories and many corridors and to have stood nearly sixty feet high, with two staircases leading to a room at its summit. If Mercury was, as has been supposed, a disguise for Adonis, it may be that here, in some ancient mystery, man tried to grant himself a glimpse of the eternal.

This fervour is the substance of Baalbec: the surge of Semitic faith through classical harmony. Men built not to please their fancies but to fulfil their souls, and stood up their needs in stone, and consecrated them. The goddess has touched everything, radiating from her sanctuary, which stands more complete than any in Lebanon. It is raised on a podium, as the Semites liked to build, and its cella is still standing from base to roof and flanked by columns sixty-two feet high, unbroken in the north and east. I crossed sward where an outer court had been, and climbed the beautiful and pitted steps to the broken pronaos. Through the monumental gateway spread a vast and delicate

* The two towers are probably contemporary.

[119]

richness, the sun trickling down the fluted columns and kindling the stone. High up the swallows circled its loneliness, valedictory spirits, where shrubs cascaded down tiers of empty niches.

At Heliopolis, wrote Eusebius, men had 'permitted their wives and daughters to commit shameless fornication', and it is no surprise. The stones themselves are ripe. The sacrifice to Jupiter was made in silence, but for Astarte there were hymns and dancing, pipes and the clash of cymbals, libations of wine and oil. Castrated priests in women's dress fell into ecstasies and blurted riddles, while the goddess-figure stood on her throne in the deep sanctuary and looked down beneath a canopy from the height of many steps. Her head was crowned with a tower, and radiated gold; in her hands a distaff and sceptre, round her waist a girdle 'wherewith they adorn none but Aphrodite of the sky'.* The friezes for her inner shrine remain, but are without solidity, all stance and gesture, where ghostly bacchantes waltz in a swirl of horns. The steps to the throne are there too, and even its piers jutting from the wall, and the base of a pillar which had held the goddess's baldachin above her. One sees the *entasis* of the columns, subtly swelling them and the sublimating rise and depth of stairs, behind which the goddess stood, keeping the dark brilliance of her worship.

That so much survives of what is rare and fragile is a miracle. From the portico ceilings the faces of carved gods have been chipped away by the zeal of Moslem iconoclasts, but their attributes betray them: hammers, rods and sheafs of corn. They look through polygonal windows in a coffered lattice-work almost Islamic for intricacy. A Semitic starkness informs them and eastern hands have shaped their cornucopiae, their grapes and rounded breasts.

But most beautiful in Baalbec is the doorway to Astarte's temple, whose height of over forty-two feet is absorbed in the grandeur of the sanctuary. Beneath its lintel a carved eagle flies, with garlands and genii; and the ornamental bands which trace the entrance hold corn and poppies, symbols of life and death, vines and ivy interflowing and the eggs from which Aphrodite was hatched by a dove. In the arbours formed by weaving stems are many tiny supple figures which are half rubbed away. Cupids gather grapes into little baskets, and here and there have overflowed to an inner ornamental panel and are

* Lucian: *The Syrian Goddess.*

standing on the stalks of corn. All is light and fruitfulness, the dance and gaiety of earth.

But Puritans revolted against this abandon. The loveless are jealous of love, and it was because she was envious of Aphrodite that the chaste goddess Artemis, according to one version of the legend, killed Adonis in Lebanon. And it was chastity, in the reign of Constantine, which was outraged by the rites at Baalbec. The emperor, said Socrates Scholasticus, 'directed that another church should be constructed in Heliopolis in Phoenicia, . . . for the laws of the country ordered the women among them to be common, and therefore the children born there were of doubtful descent, so that there was no distinction of fathers and their offspring. Their virgins also were presented for prostitution to the strangers who resorted thither. . . .'

Against Constantine's edict the dying gods exacted a horrible revenge: 'The citizens of Heliopolis, near Mount Libanus, were exceptionally cruel. . . . They stripped the sacred virgins, who had never been seen by the people . . . disembowelled them, and hid in their viscera the food generally given to pigs; and the swine, greedy for their usual food and unable to distinguish, also tore up the human flesh.'*

This story, probably distorted during the century which elapsed between the action and its telling, assumes simple cruelty; but the undertones are curious. The 'holy virgins' were probably the temple prostitutes, and the pig was sacred to Adonis and was confused with him in the old affinity between the slayer and the slain. The priests of Heliopolis, it seems, fearful of the god's anger, were giving him back the women whom Constantine had banned from his worship.

It may be that the Christians were already regarding as indecent what the Phoenicians had always seen as the exercise of a holy faculty: the creation of new life. But the reaction of the people of Baalbec, if it has been truly chronicled, condemns them, as blind faith is condemned by humanity. In A.D. 361 the emperor Julian restored the pagan rites and a deacon who had broken up the sacred statues was killed. But the pagan day was over. 'While Constantine only shut up the temples of the Greeks,' says the Paschal Chronicle, 'Theodosius destroyed them; and likewise the temple of Balanios or Heliopolis, the great and renowned, the Three-Stoned; and converted it into a Christian church.' So a basilica was built in the Court of Sacrifice, where German archaeologists found it; but although

* Hermias Sozomen: *Ecclesiastica Historia.*

the gods were smashed, the cupids were left hanging on the doorways, and ascended the lintels with garlands and horns.

*   *   *

Outside the acropolis is a rotunda which has been called the Temple of Venus, and here too the figures remain, though faded, of a dove (perhaps) and a goddess rising from the sea in a shell. It is feminine and exquisite, a folly in a Renaissance garden. Borromini copied it for the lantern of St Ivo's in Rome, and Henry Hoare set it in replica above the lakes of Stourhead. Eusebius said that Venus was venerated at Baalbec under the name of 'Hedone', Pleasure, and that her rites were licentious; but he was referring, I feel, to the main temple of Venus-Astarte.

Around the rotunda the Roman city lies like a half-reaped field: a town where the flute-players were famous and the women beautiful. Its traces stretch across the oasis: a vanished temple, sacred to Mercury-Adonis; the Roman colonnades of the Grand Mosque, roofless among grass and poppies. And in a quarry lies the largest cut stone in the world, which the Arabs call *Hajar el Hubla*, 'the Woman with Child', sixty-nine feet long and sixteen wide, a thousand tons in weight, its chiselling uncompleted. Slowly, like a shy monster, it is creeping back into the earth, but three blocks scarcely smaller uphold the Jupiter temple in the western acropolis: the largest building materials ever used, which gave to the temple its ancient name 'Three-Stoned'.

The Moslems turned the acropolis into a fortress and hacked the cupid faces from Astarte's gateway, leaving the bodies like winged insects there. In the eighteenth century Robert Wood made his handsome drawings of the ruins in time to swell the Palladian stream in England, Lady Hester pitched her tents near the springs after the first snowfall, and Lamartine wept for his dead Julia by the temples in moonlight.

The ruins should be visited at sunset and in darkness, like any sanctuary of cosmic gods, but when I came down at dusk from the ruined temple of Mercury the gates were closed. A broken moon stood in the clouds. I took a pathway which followed the walls south and west, where the trees were gathered thickly, and stumbled in the darkness.

'Is there anything you want, mister?' a voice asked.

'No,' I said to the blackness.

'I can give you anything.' A shadow had walked across the path. 'You like to drink, to smoke?'

'No,' I said.

The shadow crept close. It smelt of garlic. The voice was Circean and mellifluous. 'I have hashish of every kind. Number-one-hash, number-two-hash and number-three-hash. And any other hash.'

The temples were ashen with moonlight. The man's voice went on whispering like water over sand: descendant from a priest of Astarte; 'wonderful dreams . . .'

He flashed photographs in front of me. 'You are English?'

'Yes.'

'I have many English friends. They all come and smoke with me. This is Smith from Liverpool. He took five kilos. And this is Barbara. Very nice girl, Barbara. We did everything together . . .'

He untied a package and crumbled the dark lumps between his fingers. I walked along the pathway, but he rose beside me again. 'If you will not buy any, here, take these!' and he pressed cigarettes into my hand. I made a move to pay for them, but there was nobody there.

'A gift,' said the voice somewhere from the further night, and hissed jubilantly: 'Number-one-hash!'

Animals grunted and whispered in the underbush, and a bird sang darkly. As I walked, the pillars of Jupiter unfolded from the sky, stark with moonlight. I lit one of the cigarettes and drew deep in honour of Astarte. The smoke became a soft canopy to move under, to pass a barbed-wire gate, to climb to the temple of the moon goddess. And there the pale sanctuary rose, with its colonnades of pearl and darkness, a low vapour round it. My feet were silent over the rocks; the stars were shining. The shadows of the columns lay like ditches among stone, and between them glades of light moved across the terraces, until it seemed that other columns stood behind, in many ranks, filling out the emptiness, as light and darkness made love with one another.

I stood in an unfamiliar portico, and passing where the moon cast serrated shadows, heard giggling and a flurry of footsteps. Looking up, I saw that on the temple pediment a statue of the goddess stood paler than alabaster. From the whole sanctuary incense was rising like a mist, and far away came the sound of cymbals and drums in a high, unearthly chanting. The sounds seemed to be swimming through the air toward me. I could no longer tell where the temple columns met the sky, for they had

[123]

multiplied in the gloom, and ascended to a penumbra of tiled roofs and statued pediments. From the whiteness of new stone the painted green and blue acanthus leaves broke shockingly along the Sacrificial Court and roofs glittered with barbaric colours.

Then the cymbals burst out with singing. In a marbled pool of light an arc of dancers knelt—Aramean girls with bangled arms and scented hair—and behind them came acolytes with flutes and horns, podgy eunuch-priests and a mob of white-clad divines, who babbled in delirium. From the pyres a hundred rams smoked up, and a hundred incense-altars shed their balm. Countless faces stared from corridors and galleries with a rumour of many tongues and the bleating of emasculate priests, and in the tower of mysteries a newly-fledged prophet let out an initiatory howl.

Walking slowly, like ivory in the moonlight, the priests ascended the steps of Astarte, and the great bronze doors, silent on their hinges, opened upon a sanctuary of muted gold. Thirty gods, draped in streaked onyx with eyes of precious stones, looked down from gilded niches, where far behind her shrine the Great Goddess stood, holy in gloom and incense. Now the dancers bent and unfurled about the temple steps and the priests fidgeted impotently, and the divines were sweating.

I could hear the cupids munching grapes along the lintels. The whole gateway was lapped in the sounds of falling fruit as the little baskets overflowed, with smacking lips and the reproving murmurs of the gods beneath their pediments. Dreamily, like snakes, the dancers caressed the paving with their anointed bodies. A marble Artemis covered herself and looked away, and a poorly Hellenized Phoenician divinity discarded his Greek chiton and slanted his sapphire eyes. From the plinths of the inner sanctuary the stone bacchantes swirled on air, joking lewdly and blowing their horns.

So the music ended and the girls ran lithely from the temple and vanished down the colonnades. From some deep cell the oracle groaned enigmatically, and a sacred swine squealed in the distance. The people were trailing away with lanterns and torches down subterranean passageways. Laughter echoed faintly in a temple annex where some Lycian youths had loitered by the rooms of the prostitute-dancers, and a bracelet tinkled on a marble floor.

I followed a priest across the Court of Sacrifice, but he disappeared, and all I could hear was the flipping of nereids in the holy pools, their fins glinting; and once a triton rose with a gurgle beside me and gasped, and put its finger to its lips, and sank again.

Then, already far away, I heard the cymbals dying with the noise of falling rain, and saw the lights dimming in the shrines, the last ripples of the pools smoothing, and temple columns broken in the sky.

12. Against the Stranger

> I am against my brother; my brother and I are against my cousin; cousin, brother and I are against the stranger.
>
> *Lebanese proverb*

THE LAND WAS DYING, as the ancients said it died; the sun had worn the valleys brown and drunk the streams. I walked with relief toward the mountains, dreaming of the sea which was beyond, and of Byblos. From the furrows a single column grew, and here and there a Roman had marked on a rock the boundaries of his land, at a time when it was more fertile: 'C. Coraco', 'Utinia Cornelia'. It is said that there are places of sacrifice on the Banaat hill which juts into the western valley, but I could not find them although the wind blows through a shattered temple and rolls the blocks along its slopes.

My track petered out among foothills where the villagers of Chlifa had wired it against the people of Yammouneh, with whom they have an old feud. These are independent hills, crossed with many invisible boundaries, where grazing rights have been disputed for centuries in blood and a shepherd from afar can tell a man's village from the way he walks. But nobody was to be seen along the oak-spotted glens.

I found the road which the Romans paved between their cities at Yammouneh and Baalbec. In the plains the farmers have spread the fields above it, but through the solitary valley it wound with a cobbled brightness by empty, defensive passes beyond which the mountains rose in a low plume of clouds. Cream-coloured sheep-hounds reared savagely from vantage-points in the rocks, and I saw a fortress-village, the hashish crop young in its fields, and men with guns walking on the crags.

Along the track the flowers were dying, leaving the maquis brutal, with a host of shrubs whose airy, ciliate stems waved and rasped across the stones: juniper trees, cistus and many spiny, aromatic plants, with arbutus whose wood is used for flutes; and here and there anemones had wilted and dropped their petals one by one, Adonis already dying.

The Roman road curled under shadows, where the hills had a

strong, unfinished look. I almost trod on a tortoise, thinking him a rock, and he waved his arms at me, opening his red mouth as if to cry. At last the High Lebanon rose cold and steep as a wall, the village of Yammouneh in the valley against it, and a river shone blindingly where the sun struck it in a scimitar. My feet sent tiny pebbles rolling down the track, and I was surprised, looking at the far village, that it was silent and the fields empty, the whole valley in suspension.

A pair of armoured cars stood in the orchards, a platoon of soldiers among tents. They stared at me in astonishment. I presented my papers to their officer who was friendly but bewildered.

'How did you get here?'

I indicated the Roman road.

'You *walked*?'

He seemed to think me harmless but mad.

'Where will you sleep tonight?'

I nodded toward the village. 'Over there.'

'*There?*'

'Yes.'

He looked perplexed. 'You realize the situation?'

'Yes,' I said, thinking that he meant the state of alert over Israel. He returned my papers to me.

'Go then, but if you have any trouble, come down to us here.'

I reached the village outskirts. Hens were pecking grain in the streets and there was nobody to be seen, no children, no old men in the doorways. The front entrances to many houses were shuttered with iron, and a wind was throwing dust along the paths. I began to walk quietly; I had heard that Yammouneh was the fiercest village in Lebanon. Then I glimpsed a woman with a pitcher, and other women were peering at me from the rooftops. They did not move.

The only man I saw was standing in the shadow: a monkey-faced farmer dressed in satanic black. He asked me to his home, but quietly, as if afraid of being overheard, and we slunk along walls where the soldiers below could not see us, and entered his house by a back way. The wind had pierced his ears and he sank moaning onto the floor, holding his head in his hands, but after a while he sat up and cursed and grinned, and his wife brought him medicine, and food for me. She was good-looking, like the Bedawi, and did her housework with a two-year-old child on her shoulder, perched like a gremlin with his fingers twined in her hair. Their two-roomed house was bare and very clean, with rugs piled by the walls, a few jars, an oil lamp and a cabinet of precious odds and ends.

'I am Abbas Charife,' the man said. 'My home is yours.' For a while he smoked, watching me and pondering. 'You saw the soldiers?'

'They let me through.'

He made all sorts of gestures with his hands. 'A few days ago we had a battle against the villagers of Akura. An old affair. We killed two of them. One was shot outright and the other died on the edge of his orchard. The soldiers are trying to get us. They want every man of the Charife family, and *everybody* in this village is called Charife. We are cordoned off. How did *you* get here?'

'By the eastern track, through Chlifa.'

'You are lucky.' He assumed that the soldiers would have shot at me. I said it would be bad manners to kill a foreigner.

'Already half our men are prisoners. The soldiers have taken them to Beirut. They raided us at night and trapped us in our houses, and only twenty escaped; so now we sleep in the mountains. But at day we must till our crops or we will starve, so we come down at dawn and watch the soldiers if they move. When the winter arrives the snow will lie so thick here that maybe they will go; they only have tents. Then perhaps everything will be forgotten again.'

The Yammounites have feuded with their neighbours for years over plots of barren land, so Abbas spoke matter-of-factly, accepting a few killings as a part of life. The special enemy is the Christian village of Akura on the far side of the mountains. There had been Christians once in Yammouneh too, but they had fled, leaving an empty church at one end of the village. Abbas regarded their flight with derision. 'I suppose it is true,' he admitted, 'that a few of them were killed; but nobody asked them to *leave*.'

He lay back on a mattress and swathed his keffieh round his aching ears, while his wife sat by the window and gave her milk to the child, making a very gentle, biblical tableau in the dying sunlight, with the dark beauty of her hair and breast.

At nightfall the Charifi assembled in the room with their cartridge belts strapped round them. They were open and boisterous, but as Moslems they were abstemious, and though the hashish which they grew might be smuggled on camel-back across the mountains to the sea, they never tasted it. We talked into the night about the early caliphate and the rifts in Islam, and ate the mountain meal of *lebne, markouk* bread and apple jam, squatting round the lantern light with the doors and windows bolted.

Later they became afraid that the soldiers would trap them, and Abbas, ashamed, said that they must leave for the hills. 'The soldiers may make a raid. If they knock you must let them in; but there won't be any fighting. They will find only a village full of women, and you.'

He shuffled his feet miserably, unsure of what was right, since there was no precedent for a foreigner sleeping alone in a village full of Moslem women. His wife went out with a lantern into the street and returned after a while and whispered something; and the men clasped my hand one by one and went into the night, the scrape of their boots fading on the rocks. The woman dimmed the lantern and brought in her mother, and they lay down to sleep in their working clothes, as Arab peasants do, and I stretched out among the cushions by the wall, waiting for the knocking on the door.

But morning came peacefully and I met Abbas by the Yammouneh lake, which the French had almost drained away thirty years before to irrigate the Beqaa. The water which tumbles from the hill is called 'the Spring of Forty Martyrs', for the villagers claim that it starts to flow every ninth of March on the Feast of the Forty Martyrs, and dries up on the last day of July. There is a temple here, formless in the pastel quiet of trees and water, made of heavy Roman blocks and dedicated to Astarte, whose holy lake it is; for Phoenician legend says that she fled here from the monster Typhon and changed herself into a fish.

From the Adonis valley on the far side of the mountain, Phoenician pilgrims came to purify themselves in the sacred waters, and the Romans cut a road along their way. Fish were holy to the goddess and were perhaps kept in the lake, for Lucian mentions fish in the lake of the Mother Goddess at Hierapolis so tame that they came when they were summoned; and one remembers the god-fish which Xenophon found at Chalus near Aleppo, and many others scattered over the eastern Mediterranean.

During the last century the archaeologist Ernest Renan found sections of pediment and frieze from the Yammouneh temple, and the statue of a vegetation god was discovered too, a Roman version of Adonis, cradling a lamb in his left arm. Recently a tractor churned up a cockleshell niche from the rubble and sculptured inside was a goddess with outspread arms. But although the niche remained, the machine had smashed the head and left the body broken.

For centuries villagers have used the Roman pass through the mountains to the Adonis valley as a secret passage. If I had taken it, I might have reached, in a few hours, the heart of this holy country and the end of the quest. It was strange to be so near. But the villagers said that the soldiers were strung in a cordon along the crags. 'They are waiting for us to attack the Akurans again,' said Abbas, 'or for the Akurans to take revenge. They might shoot on sight.' The mountains there were trackless and steep, ethereal with snow, keeping their secret. So I had to find the valley by circling round to Byblos and the sea, as I had first intended, and contented myself with paddling numbly in Astarte's holy waters which the Yammounites believe to flow underground into the Adonis river.

I said good-bye to Abbas and made him a gift of a small knife, which he turned over in his hands unsmiling. I started along the gaunt valley, and looking back, saw the soldiers deploying across the road towards the houses. But from a wall one woman called 'Salma, some guests are here . . .' and the cry went from rooftop to rooftop, innocent and bird-like, so that already the men would be slipping back into the mountains.

I approached the Christian hamlet of Ainata and knew from a distance that something had happened. The street was filled with men and boys, who stared at me so bemused that I had almost passed before a burly man stopped me. 'You realize there's a war on? Egypt, Syria and Jordan attacked Israel an hour ago. Lebanon is in it too.'*

They crowded round me without smiling or enmity, but with a kind of stifled pity which frightened me.

'You must avoid Moslem villages,' said the man. 'They will be mad now. They might kill you. They say the English are the allies of Israel. In each place you come to, look for this'—he pointed to the church belfry—'and you know you will be safe. If you see a minaret, go the other way.'

'I'll walk over the mountains,' I said. I pointed where a track, engineered by the French army, stretched up the valley face and vanished under whiteness high above. 'Over there it's Christian country.'

'But there's nothing but snow,' the man said. 'Fifty kilometres

* In fact it was Israel who had attacked, shortly before eight o'clock that morning, 5th June 1967.

before the nearest village. It may be impassable. Nobody has come over yet this year.'

I said that I would try it, not believing that the snow, even after the hard winter, could still smother the track. And I felt relief as I looked up at its beauty—the spine of Lebanon—for it is easier to risk nature, whose hazards are innocent, than the hostility of man.

So I started up the track until the Beqaa valley was grand and remote below, and a cartload of nomads, moving to some upper pasture, caught up with me and hoisted me onto their folded black tents with chickens, umbrellas and corn-headed children. They were Christians, and tried to sell me a jewelled cross which a beautiful girl kept in a scarf; and one of the men offered to buy my boots.

Eventually the cart-wheels on one side were breaking down the ledges of snow, and on the other skirting the dizzy rim of the valley so that we were forced to halt, and the nomads pitched camp in a hollow and I left them. After a long time the track lifted to the summit of the range, then vanished, and ahead in folds and crescents as far as I could see glimmered virgin snow-fields. The only sound was the sharpness of the wind in my ears. My feet were silent on the supernatural earth, and the knolls and plains below were carved from mist. The steep, soft snow-packs and the sky's paleness became fused together, as if all motion and colour had been wrung out of those inviolate hills.

I felt a light, vague fear, only articulate in my body, while my mind was lost in the strangeness of the mountains, impersonal as an empty planet. Where the ice sloped suddenly to rocks I crawled on hands and knees, following the path where I imagined it lay, fifteen feet below. The sun had softened the surfaces, and by digging in my heels I made a slow progress, leaving weird tracks and sometimes resting and unfreezing my fingers where the sun had melted the snow and purple swathes of flowers broke, like mattresses for kings.

Into the noon silence, from an invisible height, came a whining like mosquitoes. A few minutes later something exploded faintly in the valley, and to the south sounded a hollow, passionate thumping as if someone were beating a drum beyond Hermon. But all these notes—the guns from the Syrian heights and the dying of an Israeli aeroplane—fell with an unreal and miraculous clarity on the mountain wind. And by late afternoon I was astride the High Lebanon; to the east lay the Moslem valleys, the foothills hiding Syria and imagined deserts, while to the west, wave upon wave, the Christian mountains rose through blueness like atolls on a hazy sea.

Soon I could see the Old Grove of cedars, more than four hundred, but pitifully small at the head of the valley, and came down to a shop and a locked hotel. I found shelter with a gang of Syrian road-menders in a bare building nearby. An old man slept on a board in one corner of a room and was startled to awake and find me lying on the floor beside him. He cooked a cauldron of beans and we sat in the fading light, eating them in silence: the first day of war. Later twenty or thirty young men came in, but the reports issuing from Radio Cairo were making the downing of Israeli planes seem like a royal grouse-shoot, and they were jubilant and forgot to resent me.

'Egypt has shot down sixty-eight planes, Jordan twenty, Syria eleven, Lebanon four!' Martial music followed the messages. Then the voice would speak again and the roadmen would cheer and shake my shoulder good-naturedly as I tried to sleep.

'News! Egypt has now shot down seventy, Jordan twenty-one, Syria eleven, Lebanon four!'

I asked them to switch to the B.B.C. and they did; for a moment there was only crackling.

'They are machine-gunning the B.B.C.,' someone said.

Then from the circle of swarthy faces the notes of Big Ben rose one by one with an exotic majesty. The Overseas Service. I interpreted: 'Israel claims to have pressed back Egypt in the Gaza strip. . . .' Faces fell. But mostly the news was so vague as not to be news. All was conjectural or contradictory. The road-menders shrugged and switched to Beirut which gave instructions for black-out and for action when bombs were falling in the streets.

I went out while it was still evening and tried to find a last hour of peace, walking beneath the cedars. The grove is not the largest in Lebanon, but the oldest, and about twelve of its great trees are thought to have lived fifteen hundred years. The peasants call them 'Arz er-Rab', 'the Cedars of the Lord', and say that Christ and His Apostles left their staves behind them on the slope and that they flowered into trees. Now a divinity inhabits the grove, and anyone who cuts the boughs for firewood is cursed. Winter had broken down many branches, which lay ungathered among husks and the last snow. The Maronites have built a chapel and set an altar in the valley which is the spiritual centre of their church, and every August they hold Mass, acknowledging some holiness in the sculptural trees, their chanting and incense commemorative of other rites and peoples, whose 'children remember their altars and their groves by the green trees upon the high hills'.

In ancient times spirits might be incorporate in trees, like the Greek hamadryad who died beneath the woodman's axe; or they might be lured out like the Russian wood-demons and the shy sycamore-gods of Egypt. But the Christians feel, more subtly, that God pervades the cedars, rather as do the Nosairis, who worship in holy groves on the Syrian hills in unbroken tradition from the Phoenicians, whose 'first men consecrated the plants of the earth, and judged them gods . . . .'*

Where religion permitted, the Phoenicians cut down the cedars and floated them to Egypt from Byblos three thousand years before Christ. They were used in the tomb-chambers of the early pharaohs, and their resin was precious for embalming the dead and preserved papyri so well that the sacred books of Rome, coated in *cedria*, were said to have survived five hundred years beneath the ground.

The cutting of the forests was the privilege of kings; of David, who raised a palace of cedarwood; and of Solomon's 'fourscore thousand hewers in the mountains', who floated the trunks to Joppa for his temple so that 'the cedar of the house within was carved with knops and open flowers: all was cedar; there was no stone seen'.†

Even the Assyrians built their shrines with the dark, incorruptible wood; Babylonians dedicated it to Marduk, and Persians set its beams in Persepolis. Later the Romans harvested the forests for their navy, leaving markers of inscribed stone among the severed trunks. The Byzantines cut them for churches, the Arabs for boats, and Justinian, after a long search, found a small grove for the roof of the Basilica of the Virgin in Jerusalem. As recently as the First World War the Turks were felling cedars to lay the Hejaz railway; but goats, nibbling the shoots, had killed the new forests at their birth.

Even in the Old Grove a sixteenth-century traveller found only twenty-four ancient trees; Maundrell, at the end of the seventeenth century, saw sixteen, and successive visitors recorded contradictory but declining figures until Burton reported nine, and the Maronite chapel derelict, with 'the holy

* Eusebius: *Praep. Evang.* i. 10
† I Kings vi. 18. Fir and juniper may also have been included here under the word 'cedar'.

elements placed in a sardine-box'. Later, hearing that the cedars were in danger of extinction, Queen Victoria paid for a wall to be run around them—the base of the limestone enclosure of today.

At dusk I heard distant aeroplanes and listened to the Syrians shuttering their windows. It was night when I came back to the rooms and forgetting which was mine, groped along passages, striking matches where the men sprawled close together and moaned at the light. I noticed my rucksack in the corner of a room now crowded, and the old man awoke and offered me his board, but the tiled floor was as soft. I opened a shutter, the place being without light, and lay for a long time looking at the sky, and wondering how many people had been killed that day.

*   *   *

The next morning I found a lorry going to Tripolis and a bus for Beirut. Helicopters were dropping leaflets on the city, and a muffled rifle-fire sounded from the American embassy where students were attacking troops. A note from the British embassy awaited me: 'British subjects in Syria, Lebanon, Iraq and on the East Bank of Jordan are advised that in view of the tense situation they should make preparations to leave at short notice.' The note was twelve days old.

In the little hotel I began to understand what it must have been like for the besieged in a castle. Hostility, imagined and genuine, surrounded us. Faces which had smiled were now turned away or pretended not to see: the little slights of war. It is the dilemma of Lebanon that she is almost equally divided between Christian and Moslem, and there were fears of religious unrest or of a civil war, as in 1958. The Christians began to leave for their mountain villages.

In the hotel, national qualities were accentuated. The Germans and Swedes drank and grew sullen. The British joked awkwardly. The Americans agitated for something to be done; but the harbour and the airport were closed and there was rioting round the British and United States embassies. The pivots of security had been struck away so suddenly that it was bewildering to see how frailly they were grounded: the servants bowed and left for the hills; the official was apologetic, hopeless; banks, airlines, travel agencies all shook their heads in regret.

On the second night the United States embassy organized a massive airlift and began herding its nationals into the American University compound, protected by Lebanese soldiers and armoured cars; in this ghetto atmosphere there seemed something final in the farewells to friends, and after more than three thousand had departed, the foreign sector fell silent, so that one could drive along the streets alone.

The absence of old faces unnerved those who were left. There were rumours of other ways out: Greek cargo boats which did not exist; company air flights; a bus over the Syrian border. And the conversations followed a similar vein:

'Heard anything?'

'No.'

'Where's S—?'

'He was going on an embassy flight.'

'It never came in.'

'I heard there's a Turkish boat leaving for Cyprus tonight.'

'Cancelled.'

'Where's M—?'

'Don't know. Somebody said there's rioting in the Place des Canons. . . .'

For a few hours next day the airport opened while special flights scattered foreigners round the eastern Mediterranean. The remaining British went from the hotel and only two familiar faces were left: a Canadian professor, and an American spinster who was rather deaf and would insist, when she heard housewives beating carpets in the morning, that 'The soldiers are shooting down at the embassy again.' The Canadian kept losing his glasses and I would catch myself chewing casually, with nothing in my mouth.

The war in Beirut happened in people's minds. There was little to show for it in actions. The Shell oil installation was destroyed near the harbour, probably by Palestinian refugees, and the Mobil depot blew up with a disgruntled roar. There were sporadic attacks on the embassies, where cars were burnt and people wounded, and Moslem riots after Friday prayer. But the army's control of the city was efficient and determined. The foreign and Jewish quarters were picketed by military police, who sat entrenched behind the railings of villa gardens and patrolled the streets at night, when the black-out was so effective that they bumped into lamp-posts.

There was an eloquent contrast between the crowded, effervescent Moslem quarter and the quietness of the Christian one. In the large hotels the deck-chairs were still ranged in the sun about the swimming-pools, but nobody was to be seen there. The five-hundred-room Phoenicia was occupied by twenty people, mostly from Damascus embassies, and its great escalator moved up and down in darkness.

The Moslems reacted as the Arabs like to, with fervent decision. They were jubilant and bellicose. But the Christians, who equally distrust Nasser and dislike Israel, were muted and circumspect. Their fear of becoming a tiny minority in a united Moslem world, of Egypt eventually dominating Lebanon, is kept sharp by the disaffection of the Moslems who prevail in the cities: Tripolis, Sidon, Tyre, half Beirut. Their commerce and their tourist trade had foundered, and this they bewailed with a Phoenician common sense.

Those first three days might have been years. Bewilderment changed to loneliness, then to emptiness of feeling. The long walk among mountains, and the peasant quietness, seemed irrecoverable. It was decadent to find significance in anything but the tragic present. History was all around us now. There was no meaning left in cities ruined by more ancient wars, or in the intimations of what men had once believed. And my stay might have to end prematurely, the war-god obstructing the quest.

*   *   *

The tone of Radio Cairo turned from claims of glorious victory to a note of valiant defence. With bewildering suddenness it was over. First Jordan, then Egypt, asked for peace. I was sitting in the hotel lobby when the Canadian professor came downstairs with a radio. President Nasser was 'offering his resignation'; his voice, strangely calm, choked and faltered at the end, and there was a long silence before military music broke in.

The hotel manager bolted the iron doors. An hour later I thought I heard something, but so confused and far away that it was like a wind stirring. The professor and I climbed onto the hotel rooftop. The night seemed to be holding its breath. But wherever people had painted their windows too thinly for black-out, indigo patterns showed, as if the whole bright city lay under a dark sea. From where the lightless Moslem quarter spread, came a low, wordless soughing. For over an hour it grew louder. Then, slowly, the chanting came toward us, sometimes fading to a sigh until we half believed we had imagined it, then charged with a deep, rhythmic threat. Even as it came nearer it was impossible to tell how many voices composed the roar: 'Nah-seer! Nah-seer! Nah-seer!'

Nasser. The anger of the Arab world. The plea of Palestinian refugees from the memory of their homes, which the wind shuffled between the sounds of passion and dream. They pleaded outside the Egyptian embassy, then moved into the Christian and foreign quarters and appeared to be marching on us personally, until we saw the lights of their torches along the streets ahead of them, and heard the explosions and tinkling of gutted buildings along their route: Kodak, Austin, Coca-Cola, the Russian trade delegation.

Now the whole sector was filled with lights and shouting. Some of the Christians came onto their balconies and clapped faintly. I had driven a car to Lebanon in the spring, and it was parked in the darkness of trees under the hotel, and when the torches were within a hundred yards I prepared to go down to drive it away. But the mob was diverted to dynamite a Ford Company building, then moved away toward the sea where the long-suffering embassies stood.

The night closed behind them. Figures in business suits, who had been standing silent on the rooftops, padded indoors, and little by little the city returned to quietness under the indifferent stars.

On the last day of war we were so complacent that when Israeli bombers flew over the city we stood on the verandahs to see if they would drop anything. But they were circling to attack the outskirts of Damascus, thundered low and vanished, leaving the pigeons in clouds like rubbish above the roofs. Syria accepted peace the same afternoon, and Lebanon, whose aggression had been slight and controlled, was forgotten. So the war ended before we had grown used to it, and as curfew lifted and the dawn call to prayer hung still sinister and beautiful on the air, I slid out through the Palestinian sector and went back into the hills.

13. The Holy Valley

Rich fragments of divine remembrances,
Where prophets in ecstatic vision caught
The songs of heaven,
               . . . and far above,
The Sannin's everlasting crown of snow
Blends its white splendours with the beaming sky.
                              Anon: *Lebanon,* 1819

THE GORGES OF THE ABU ALI, like most young formations,
are steep and sudden, disclosing a geologist's playground of
yellow, brown and soft-red strata. Sometimes they reach a depth
of seventeen hundred feet, where waterfalls glide and vanish,
like lances thrown into darkness. Shedding and accumulating
many horizons, the road turns dreamily above the chasm. The
cedars stand deserted in the valley-bowl, and seeing them again,
I knew that I had returned, and planned to go down the gorge
for two days to Tripolis, and reach Byblos along the sea.

But now I felt cut off from the people, as if an old trust had
been betrayed. Young men loitered under the church of
Hadchit, and a nun smiled at me on the steps; but they had
become features in a landscape, and I think of them in this way
still: the young men ageless; the nun with her rosary, smiling
and fixed in time. Even the farmers were statues in the sunlight,
and the flowering and the dying of the oleanders in the valley
seemed no more in a procession of hours than beads which may
be shuffled on a string.

But the country was radiant. For when death is remembered,
life becomes most precious, and without death, would lose its
meaning. I looked on the landscape freshly because of the war's
depression, and the old things were renewed, so that I thought
of the words of the psalmist, to whom Lebanon was beauty and
fragrance:

'He sendeth the springs into the valleys, which run among the
hills. . . . Thou makest darkness, and it is night: wherein all the
beasts of the forest do creep forth. . . . The sun ariseth, they
gather themselves together, and lay them down in their dens.

Man goeth forth unto his work and to his labour until the evening.'*

The whole canyon holds its spell from sea to mountains like a meditation on the majesty of God, and finds its end in the Wadi Kadisha, the 'Holy Valley', where between rock and air Byzantine monks built monasteries, and hermits scooped their grottoes from the cliffs.

The Maronites, shrinking from persecution, made the chasm their spiritual citadel, and all the villages which dangle on its rim and the convents in the valley are theirs. Only dependent on the Turks in name, their society was feudal but democratic: a sprinkling of tiny sees, speaking Syriac into the last century. From the time of Louis IX they have claimed friendship with France, and the closeness of their church to Rome gave them a special status in the eyes of the West. They are a tough people, nimble in the crags, and their villages, with ogival windows and ar-caded façades, looked strange and frail on the edge of the abyss.

Their spiritual ruler, 'the Patriarch of Antioch and All the East', still has his summer residence in the valley at Diman; but when I wandered its halls I saw only a group of children with archaic smiles, and a sleepy priest, whose beard smelt of incense long after divine service. He told me that a pathway descended the gorge from Hadchit. Here a man may talk across space with a villager in Hasroun, but will have to walk two hours around the valley if he wishes to shake hands.

From the church at Hadchit the chanting and cymbals of the Maronite liturgy sounded pagan on the air. The Roman Mass has changed their worship, but the rites for feast days are old and may have retained, here and there, a Phoenician shadow. On Good Friday, in the service of *jennaz*, 'burial', an effigy of the dead Christ is laid on a bier among flowers, as the image of Adonis was, and is placed in a 'tomb' beneath an altar south of the nave, and resurrected at Easter.†

So my descent into the Christian valley was not a diversion, but a return to the years of Byzantium, when the crown of Astarte was placed on the head of the Virgin in the ikons of the empire. I followed an immemorial path, worn smooth by no design other than the steep demand of the valley face and the upsurge of stray rocks, and the sun, touching the cliffs, lit up their freckled colours among empty, inaccessible caves.

* Psalm civ.
† These ceremonies subsist, in many forms, throughout the Eastern Church.

Somewhere in the thuya trees I heard a rustle and saw a man leaping like a faun down the rocks toward me, his feet noiseless in moccasins. Slender and smiling he stood in front of me with a gun in his hands.

'I'm Fouad.'

'I'm Colin.'

'Where are you going?'

'To look at the shrines.'

'You have already passed one. Follow and I will show you.'

We climbed through thickets over spindly streams, Fouad's movements silent except for the hunting-bag which bounced against his back. A fortress-chapel appeared above us, built crudely and entered through a high natural arch and a broken doorway. Inside was a ruined, two-apsed shrine, tucked into the cave with mud bricks and half-hewn stones, fragile as dust.

'This is Deir es Salib,' said Fouad. 'The Monastery of the Cross. The Crusaders had it but the Arabs cut off their heads.' He sawed at his throat with one hand. 'And they took out the eyes of the angels.' He pointed to the apses, and here the frescoed saints stared blindly from the shiny plaster, miraculous in their existence, each differentiated according to tradition and holding a shield in his hand. The inscribed estrangelo Syriac, if I could have read it, might have told their names; one wore the surcoat and red cross of the Knights Templars, but most were obliterated and all were dateless, with here a fount of wreathed and falling hair, there a scroll or a blistered hand raised in blessing. Near the door was an Annunciation, and St Barbara with a child.

Fouad stood in the cave entrance and pointed to where the sanctuaries of Mar Sarkis and Mar Bahonna were dimples in the rock.

'I have placed a candle in every shrine in the valley,' he said, looking back to the chapel floor which was pocked with holes. 'People found treasure down there. The gold of a king's daughter. There's other gold in the shrines, if only one knew where.'

As we walked, bending under trees and sliding down banks to find the old track, his mind was filled with stories of old feuds, and mine with a more distant past, so that we went between the same cliffways, but each knowing a different landscape: here, perhaps, some ancestor of Fouad had died, and in the cave beyond a band of Douahi had ambushed some Frangieh, and his father had found gold. But in the same places I sensed the hermits rattling their semantra, and heard Byzantine footsteps on the penitential way. So we thrust our path through greenness to Mar Antun Bedawi, and I was astonished again by the frailty of these chapels, this one a few paces long, but complete and mediaeval, with a tiny arcade and vaulted roof, guarded by the piety of stray hunters.

Fouad lit his candle while a spell of insects rose about us, and we went out into the sunlight again by a broken grotto where St Anthony of Padua is supposed to have slept. Even in the last century madmen were brought to the shrine, where a priest beat them on the head with a shoe. If they remained insane they were chained to the rock by their necks and the priest, visiting them every few days, would feed them a little and give them the sacred water which falls from the ceiling, until either they died or the iron collar fell from them. But a traveller wrote that the collars were so made as to open at a twitch of the body, and that the madmen, waking to find themselves freed, believed that St Anthony had come to them in the night.

After a few miles Fouad left, but first scratched in the ground a diagram of the way to Kannoubin, the cave-monastery which is the soul of the Maronite world. I followed streams down corridors of trees, until I walked in sun along the valley bed.

Glensides, discoloured in the seep of rain, were hacked or made smooth by man and the river; while fir and poplar trees grew with a pygmy thrust against the vivid mountains, stepping out of mist into sunlight, and back again to mist and satin shadows. High above were half-walled caves where the last anchorites died a century ago, and other caves whose entrances were bound in stalactites as if insects had kneaded them in their bodies; all sloping down gently with a premonition of the sea.

In 1820 Kannoubin lost its primacy of the Maronite world, and Burckhardt said that the patriarchs could no longer travel there in summer because of the insults of the Moslems along their way. Now it is empty, dangling like a wasps' nest on the cliffs, defensive in its solitude and age and the mysterious immortality of ill-cut stones.

Its guardian—a robust woman—lived in a dark hall where silkworms lay on mulberry leaves like animated twigs, soundlessly munching and waving their heads. The silk trade has almost vanished from Lebanon, but fifty years ago the Kadisha was full of the tall kiosks, and peasants hung bags of silkworm eggs in the chapels for a blessing.

The woman came with keys to the Grotto of St Marina and opened it. Years ago the dead Maronite patriarchs were embalmed here and seated on thrones in their sacerdotal robes; but later they stood in glass-topped coffins along the walls, and were recently sealed in an alabaster tomb. The chapel is carved from the grotto where the half-legendary St Marina lived—a virgin clothed as a monk, who saved a dying child with her miraculous milk; and women whose milk has run dry come to her altar and tend her candles.

The guardian had no key to the patriarchate, but I climbed the wall and unbolted the gate from within, and she opened the church doors for me in the overgrown courtyard. It held the essence of the whole valley: the marriage of desolation and reverence; the weeds grown to the lintels, but every stone in place. The wildness of the gorge, which once attracted monks, has left it priestless now, and the candles in the shrines are offered only by the mountaineers.

The vault of Kannoubin whispers to the flight of bats, and along its corridor open cells, empty and savage, with iron-grilled windows cut across the mountain-face. Theodosius the Great, it is said, founded it in the fourth century, eleven hundred years before it became the Maronite patriarchate. The rock-cut church, with its Byzantine apse and niches cut into the mountain, may be of his time, with the cell above its entrance where Patriarch Douahi, in the seventeenth century, wrote the classic history of his church.

The Deisis in the apse is old but not Byzantine, relaxed and curvaceous, with a sombre richness imparted by its darkened paint; perhaps a sixteenth-century work. The Christ is huge and animate, unspiritual, flanked by St Stephen, and the Virgin clad in scarlet, gold and royal blue like a mediaeval châtelaine.

On the north wall she is crowned in fresco, for the church is dedicated to her, and sits coyly among cherubim, while the Father and the Son hold the coronet above her and the Maronite patriarchs stand at her feet in massed and flaking adoration. The mural, overcrowded and too easy, is still a little touching. The guardian smiled and knelt to it.

By the wall, in a glass-lidded coffin, lay the mummified body of some unknown dignitary dug up from the chancel floor. I asked who he was, but the woman shrugged, pushing the box further against the wall, and said 'Just a body'; which I found callous for a moment, then thought it wholesome in her to have knelt before the Mother of Life, but treated dust as dust.

*   *   *

I climbed to the road again. Becharé, where the poet Khalil Gibran is buried, was left behind, and I missed the mediaeval church of Ehden, whose people claim descent from Crusaders and whose cedars, said Ezekiel, were once 'the choice and best in Lebanon'.

At dusk I made camp in the hills, where frogs mourned at night, and awoke to the sun. Already the valley was silenced by its strokes, the rocks too hot to touch; only the lizard, filling his throat with the June air, raised his head in an inaudible call. For a few hours I walked beside the road to Tripolis, where infant bracken curled, then lay in the shadow, my pack heavy with food which I never used, so generous are the mountaineers, and slept again before creeping on in the heat, like a sick hermit, to the sea. A little girl, standing by the road, thrust into my arms a bunch of anchusa and ran away without waiting for my thanks. I sat on the dazzling stones with the flowers beside me, already dying because there was no water near, and felt half sad that this impulse to give, and the purple flowers, were spent on me.

Past Arjes and Ejbeh I saw the sea, and Tripolis at the land's fingertips, the road as on a map, crossing the plain from oleandrous hills. I passed a military check-point near Zghorta, still notorious for its blood-feuds. It is perhaps the Gigarta from which Ituraean bandits raided the plains, so that Pompey, said Strabo, 'destroyed these fastnesses, from whence the robbers overran Byblos, and Berytus' and gave the town to Sidon.

Tripolis then was already old. Important temples were raised to Astarte and to Zeus Hagios, a form of Adonis, and from its three walled quarters the Greeks called it Tripolis, 'Three Cities', the Arabic 'Trablus'. Late in the seventh century the Byzantine emperor evacuated its people in ships by night and left it to the Arabs, who moved a colony of Jews there; and such was the advantage of its position that it continued to flourish, with pasturelands of sugar-cane, and harbours for a thousand ships.

The Crusaders found it deep in orchards, a town of twenty thousand people, mostly Shia Moslems, who came out to attack but were defeated, and bought their liberty with gold and horses. But Raymond of Toulouse built a castle on a mound to dominate the city. 'The Mount of Pilgrims', wrote William of Tyre, 'is well fortified both by its natural site and by the skill of those who built it. From it as a base, almost daily Raymond caused new trouble to the people of Tripoli. As a result of this constant harrying, the natives of the entire district and even those who dwelt in the city were forced to pay him an annual tribute, and in all matters obeyed him as if he owned the city without dispute.'

The castle, which once stood nearly two miles from the town walls, is lapped in houses now. To the west are the minarets and offices of a new city, with the Lombard campanile of the Great Mosque, elegant and entire from a Crusader church. Many changes have touched it, but the battlements above the Abu Ali river are Crusader still, and the whole castle crowds the hill as it has always done, in high walls and shallow square towers, which give it a blank, functional look, without a curved line or salient feature. Raymond died here without seeing Tripolis surrender, but his inheritance passed to his son Bertrand, who came with galleys from the west. In 1109 the city yielded honourably to the united Crusaders after seven years of siege, but the Genoese mariners slew people in the streets and burnt down the library of Banu Ammar with its hundred thousand volumes of Persian, Greek and Arab classics.

The citadel is entered through iron-bound doors, hard for a man to move, and a Mameluke entranceway in black and white masonry. The gate beyond it was the Crusader entrance, spanning a paved passage, and inside are courts and rooms built with small, porous stones as late as Ottoman times, though Crusader blocks lie in the foundations and a chapel wall remains.

Five generations of the county of Toulouse held the Pilgrim's Mount for Christendom. A Damascene army defeated Bertrand's son outside its walls and Syrian hillsmen murdered him; but Raymond II, wrote William of Tyre, 'collected the remnant of the cavalry and with a strong body of foot soldiers in addition went up to Mt Lebanon with great valour. There he seized and carried away in chains to Tripoli as many of those men of blood, with their wives and children, as he could find.' Still a very young man, he ruled with energy and decision, and was a jealous husband to the Queen of Jerusalem's sister, Hodierna. But she was gay and wilful and her daughter Melisende, it was said, was not his. They quarrelled so bitterly that the queen came to Tripoli and took Hodierna away, but Raymond, after escorting them to the harbour, was knifed by Assassins, and the people, who esteemed him, killed every foreigner in the city.

The beautiful Melisende was betrothed to Manuel Comnenos, Emperor of Byzantium, but for political reasons he rejected her, and from sadness and dishonour she pined away. Yet in

[145]

Provençal romance she lived on as *La Princesse lointaine*, to whom the troubadour-prince Jaufre Rudel wrote his 'Amor de Lohn'. Rudel, said legend, went on crusade for her sake, and was landed weak with fever in the harbour of Tripolis, and Melisende came to comfort him in death, and passed into song as The-Princess-over-the-Waters.*

Her brother, Raymond III, was the last of the Toulouses. A cold man, cultivated and intelligent, he tried to dissuade the Crusader army from its advance on Tiberias, though his own wife was besieged there; but others persuaded the feeble King Lusignan to march. Raymond, as lord of the fief, rode in the van, and the army moved all day across the waterless hills until it was too weak to reach Tiberias lake, and he was heard to cry, 'Ah, Lord God, the war is over; we are dead men; the kingdom is finished.' The next day, as the army was surrounded by Saladin on the Horns of Hattin, the king asked Raymond to charge with the cavalry before it was too late; and he returned in shame to Tripolis, almost the last to escape. By the end of the day the red tent of the king was submerged by the Saracen charge, the Knights Templars and Hospitallers were slain, and the rest taken to Damascus, where the price of a slave became scarcely more than a pair of sandals. Raymond's wife surrendered Tiberias soon after and was sent back with honour by Saladin, and Raymond died childless the same year, his fief passing to the house of Antioch.

Tripolis was wealthy all this time, with four thousand looms for weaving silk, and a profitable trade in glass. But the kingdom waned, and in 1289 an army of Mamelukes besieged the city and the castle on Pilgrim's Mount was abandoned. The land walls were pounded with mangonels until the south-east tower collapsed and the Venetian galleys deserted. Then the Moslems poured over the rubble and put every man to the sword. A few fled in rowing-boats to the off-shore islet of St Thomas, but the Saracens swam their horses through the shallows and killed them, so that the historian Abulfeda, who visited the island soon after, was driven away by the smell of corpses.

The Moslems ruined the town on the shore so that the Crusaders might not sail back from Cyprus and settle there, and left it an insignificant port called al-Mina, now noted for its Greek sponge-divers and for the beauty of its women. But a city

* Historically it is more probable that Rudel loved Hodierna, not Melisende; but the Melisende myth has persisted.

grew up round the castle in the bones of churches and convents, and its domes and minarets cover the plain toward al-Mina.

Today the people are restless and quickly angry, orthodox Moslems who would like to join Syria, with many refugees among them. I dared enter the city only in a car, and saw that many public buildings had been burnt in rioting after the Arab defeat, and was afraid to explore the older quarters as I would have wished. The soldiers said that they could not protect me, and even in the modern streets the people stared after my car in fury and disbelief.

A man accosted me as I entered the citadel: a small, sallow man, respectably dressed, whose eyes were ill and gleaming. He seized my arms and pushed me, as if he were trying to move a wardrobe, and I stood stupidly staring at him. I handed him my papers from the Ministry of Tourism, which he held upside down and scrutinized. I tried smiling at him. At first he looked bewildered and took several paces backward; then a quiver turned his lips and he handed back my papers, holding his head and staring after me as I entered the citadel. But by the time I emerged he had forgotten his smile and had gathered several men and was trying to form a mob. I approached them slowly, affecting an interest in the vaulting of the passage-ways, amazed at how deep-rooted is the fear of losing dig-nity. I might have run or hid or squeezed myself through some postern window. Instead, mainly from a horror of looking ridiculous, I walked to the crowded gateway. Here the guardians of the citadel said that I was a harmless French archaeologist, so I smiled at all these men too and tried to look French and harmless, and while they were arguing as to what should be done, I drove away.

There are, I believe, many stones from Byzantine Tripolis immured in the mediaeval town, but I was unable to search for them, and nothing of the great Phoenician city remains. I drove to the sea where it had stood, and to the Qubbet el Bedawi, a monastery for dervishes whose site may have been sacred in antiquity. Parts of its walls are mediaeval, and according to Christian tradition the Crusaders built a priory here to St Anthony of Padua on the place of a Phoenician temple.

I felt again the nearness of the ancient world—the touching of hands between Phoenicia and Greece—and walked on the paved soil which covered old sanctities. I wandered round the eastern wall of the mosque to a wide, semi-circular pool and saw, gliding between sunlight and shadow, the holy fish of Astarte.

Their veneration goes back beyond memory and their ancestors, it is said, were here when the pool was Phoenician. They are never eaten, but are piously fed by visitors, who pour delicacies into the water, and in the last century people came to make vows to them or to receive their blessing, believing them to be inhabited by human souls.

So, even in the precincts of Islam, the champions of the older world had slyly entered. Of course it may be that the Moslems are right and that the shapes which glimmer there are human souls; but if you look carefully you will see that there is something fat and probable about them, like carp or river-bass, whose parents were pampered long ago in the courts of the Great Goddess.

Anjar: the Ommayad palace

Baalbec: the temple of Astarte ('Temple of Bacchus')

Byblos: Crusader Castle

Byblos: the Obelisk Temple

14. The City of Adonis

> Find again the sad Adonis, and lay him among crowns and flowers. All things are dead with him, as he is gone, and the plants are withered. . . .
> *Bion*

I PRESSED AT THE DOOR, and the wood and iron gave a dark, anguished shriek as they wrenched each other for a millionth time, then swung back with a sigh. Beyond were galleries of dust and faded sunlight, roofed without beams and passing to chambers where the Crusaders piled their stores and quartered men when they first built the castle over Byblos. The Arabs rebuilt the western walls, binding the light pudding-stone with ancient columns, and the Crusaders raised the keep with Roman blocks, laying them as they were found, massive and irregular.

From this height the salient of Byblos lay hypnotized between the sun and sea, dusted in mauve-pink hollyhocks, like an unkept garden. The ruins were empty of tourists, the war still too near, and this comfortable solitude seemed a part of them; for here were no living buildings, but a vague geometry beneath the scrub, excavation at the hands of friendly and knowledgeable men, with the maquis and asphodel risen again unchecked.

Seven thousand years ago, at the end of the prehistoric age, people lived exposed here in huts above the sea, traded and farmed and laid lime plaster floors as hard and polished as pebbles. There are vestiges of a temple, predicting the form of later Semitic sanctuaries—a shrine within a sacred court—and men were buried with their pottery and weapons; so early was the instinct that life did not end. You may walk along the western cliff by their village, with its low walls of unequal stone, and find the egg-shaped holes in the mud floors from which the bodies of Chalcolithic men were plucked out. The dead dwelt with the living, let into the floors in jars, where they lay jewelled with their knees drawn to their chins, ready for the realm of the Great Mother, whose idols they had carved from bone.

At the end of the fourth millennium a revolution is implied in the new order of the houses, their carefully chosen stones, the simple drainage, and graveyards set apart; and men used copper to cut down trees and stretched their hide walls from wooden columns whose perforated stone bases are scattered everywhere. Perhaps this marks the migration west of the Canaanites—the pith of the Phoenicians—whose houses, a few centuries later, had spread with ramparts over the headland, and ended the farmer's quiet living.

It is through their defences, raised from brown rocks haphazardly, that the city is entered, over stones sprung with thistles, climbing by steps to a small, sea-girt beauty of ruin. In the space of twelve and a half acres lie the patterns of seventy centuries, shrouded in the faint applause of insects, where the cramped little Canaanite houses spoilt each other's view of the sea. A temple is close, built for an unknown god on the lip of a sacred pool, now dry, its walls rough and intimate to touch and less than shoulder-high as they were first built, for the support of wood and fabrics.

It is an easy, eventless world which seems to lie here, measured by centuries and the stones' gentle confusion. The earliest Phoenicians are almost too old for history, but they traded as far as Sudan and Armenia, and floated cedars to Egypt when the pyramids were new; and their pottery, burnished and assured, arrived in the tombs of the Old Kingdom. But towards 2000 B.C. the Amorites conquered Byblos—the marks of their fires are still dark—and broke up the Canaanite streets and built a new temple on the old.

The stub of a giant obelisk, a *maseboth*, rests at its centre, and many smaller ones stood in the courtyard round it, like spectators or disciples, and are there still, squat and tapering, upright or leaning, their significance unknown. Bracelets, brooches and necklaces of twisted gold were left by the anvil of the temple jeweller; and buried in jars or immured in the foundations were offerings to Reshef, god of war—ceremonial daggers and electrum hatchets; hieratic figures snipped from gold leaf in silhouette like Indonesian puppets, mere filaments, golden shadows of men; and an army of flattened bronze warriors, corroded into pristine colours.

But an older, more important sanctuary was raised before 3000 B.C. on the far side of the sacred pool to 'The Mistress of Byblos' and outlasted the conquest until Amorite and Phoenician were one, and invaders from Egypt and the east had overlapped and receded. For three thousand years new offerings glittered in her shrine, and the pharaohs from as long ago as Cheops, builder of the Great Pyramid, sent her alabaster vases covered with their changeless symbols and inscribed with their names. They addressed her as Hathor, whom the Greeks called Aphrodite, and she was, almost surely, the earth-mother of this region, the young Astarte.

The cult of the goddess and her lover goes almost unrecorded until classical times. 'Byblos, the royal seat of Cinyrus, is sacred to Adonis. Pompey delivered this place from the tyranny of Cinyrus, by striking off his head.' So the last king of Byblos is removed from history by the sword of Pompey and the pen of Strabo. The name Cinyrus is significant, for it was given by Greek legend to the father of Adonis, and some kings of Cyprus and Byblos took it to themselves. The first Cinyrus crossed the sea to Cyprus and was loved by Aphrodite. Some said he married the daughter of Pygmalion, the island king, others that he sired Adonis by his own daughter Myrrha at a festival of Ceres, the corn-goddess; and Pygmalion himself fell in love with a statue of Aphrodite and took it to his bed. In these three generations, all linked by legend to the Great Mother, one may see, as Frazer does,* a true history of early kings who took to themselves the name and divinity of their god, and were married ritually to the goddess.

This sacred monarchy, because it descended through the female line, might require that a king marry his mother or daughter. Their children would become god-kings and queens after them, and so perpetuate the union of Astarte and Adonis, and keep in trust the riches of the earth. It seems that in early times the king was slain when he grew old, lest the harvest also weaken, and that his bones or ashes were scattered in the fields to replenish them; so he died in the way of Osiris and Attis, and of Jesus too, giving new life to men by the offering of his blood.

By classical times the divine kingship at Byblos had faded, but it had become the religious capital for all Phoenicia, a city of the gods, and lodestar for pilgrims. Astarte's temple was reached by stairs before a columned portico, and from its court an obelisk, perhaps the incarnation of the goddess, rose above the temple roof.

'I saw too at Byblos a large temple, sacred to the Byblian Aphrodite', wrote Lucian in a famous passage of *The Syrian Goddess*; 'this is the scene of the secret rites of Adonis: I

* Sir James Frazer: *The Golden Bough. Adonis.*

mastered these. They assert that the legend about Adonis and the wild boar is true, and that the facts occurred in their country, and in memory of this calamity they beat their breasts and wail every year, and perform their secret ritual amid signs of mourning through the whole countryside.'

The mysteries of Adonis have remained an enigma. Probably they developed late under Egyptian influence and reflected the open rite which laid the god in his tomb and resurrected him. 'When they have finished their mourning and wailing', says Lucian, 'they sacrifice in the first place to Adonis, as to one who has departed this life: after this they allege that he is alive again, and exhibit his effigy to the sky. They proceed to shave their heads too, like the Egyptians on the loss of their Apis. The women who refuse to be shaved have to submit to the following penalty, viz., to stand for the space of an entire day in readiness to expose their persons for hire. The place of hire is open to none but foreigners, and out of the proceeds of the traffic of these women a sacrifice to Aphrodite is paid.'*

So this prostitution, in the second century after Christ, was still an act of piety, and just as women surrendered what was female in the form of their hair or their virginity, so men castrated themselves, dedicating their power to the gods, and afterwards served in the temples as priests.

Through the eastern Mediterranean the rites varied, and the god's images, anointed and gashed in the thigh by an imaginary boar, were carried on a bier in lamenting procession, thrown into springs and rivers, floated out to sea, or placed in tombs and resurrected after days of sadness.

> The tender Adonis is dying, Cytherea. What can we do?
> Beat your breasts, maidens, and rend your garments.

This is Sappho, who gave beauty to the harsh Semitic line, and may herself have sung the Adonia.

The time of the festival was variable, but at Byblos it took place in spring. Pots of corn and flowers, called 'Gardens of Adonis', were sown on the first day of festival and fertility cones set among them. Symbolic of the god's life and death, they quickly withered and were thrown with his image into the sea as charms for harvest. The descendants of these gardens survive in country traditions from Provence to Bengal, and were known more than twenty-five centuries ago when they lured the Hebrews from the worship of Jehovah:

* Lucian: *The Syrian Goddess*. Trs. Prof. H. A. Strong.

'Because thou hast forgotten the God of thy salvation, and hast not been mindful of the rock of thy strength, therefore shalt thou plant pleasant plants, and shalt set it with strange slips:

'In the day shalt thou make thy plant to grow, and in the morning shalt thou make thy seed to flourish: but the harvest shall be a heap in the day of grief and of desperate sorrow.'*

Even in Bethlehem this worship flourished, and the first to wail by the wall of the temple in Jerusalem were the believers in Adonis. 'Then he brought me to the door of the Lord's house which was toward the north,' says the Book of Ezekiel, 'and, behold, there sat women weeping for Tammuz.'

By conjuring their emotions out of nothing, they blurred the boundaries of true feeling, until the false tears were followed by others, less conscious, and the mime of sorrow had created sorrow itself: a cry into the dark. For these were gods of death as well as life; Astarte held in her hand the pomegranate, which was a symbol of the kingdom of Persephone, though its seeds were emblems of hope.

The sadness continues all along the headland, houses and temples lost under asphodel, the flower of the dead. Early in the second millennium Amorite kings were buried beneath the acropolis down dark, chiselled passageways: kings with Babylonish names in gross sarcophagi, shaped like houses. With them were the treasures which were to keep them kings in death: ceremonial furniture, flasks and coffers in obsidian and gold; pectorals and amulets, amethyst and brecchia; a bird-headed incense-spoon, a silver Aegean vase; rich, solid works which respected their materials.

In all this is sensed the nearness of Egypt, the trade links with Mesopotamia and the Caucasus. Then the Hyksos seized Byblos with chariots and left new weapons formidable in their graves; and the city grew, overlapped its walls and built wider ramparts. Figurines show a fresh attempt at naturalness. Dogs' and rams' legs are set shyly in motion, and Egyptian beasts appear soon after, child's creations still—gnomic gods with dictatorial hands, hundreds of supple-armed monkeys, humorous cats and graceful women.

By the eighteenth century before Christ the Egyptians had control of the city, and did not lose it until the siege of the Hittites three hundred years later, when the piteous letters of its vassal king went unanswered by the pharaohs. 'Like a bird

* Isaiah xvii. 10, 11.

[153]

that is caught in a snare, so am I in this city of Gebal.* . . . If no help comes, then am I a dead man.'

For centuries Byblos stood nervous on the rim of the Egyptian power. Ramses II built a monument to himself here and gave gifts to Ahiram its king, whose sarcophagus was sunk in thirty feet of rock on the low necropolis. Women who mourn in bas-relief upon it, and the sculptured tribute-bearers to the king, invest it with a wan Egyptian glory; but it rests upon Hittite lions with tame, foreshortened faces. Carved on the shaft of the sepulchre were the words 'Warning, thy death lies below', and a curse was inscribed on the sarcophagus itself in letters ancestral of our own alphabet, which we owe to the Phoenicians:

'Itobaal, son of Ahiram, king of Gebal, made this sarcophagus for Ahiram, his father, as his dwelling for eternity. And if a king among kings, or a governor among governors, raises war against Gebal and lays bare this sarcophagus, the sceptre of his power will be broken, the seat of his royalty will be overthrown, and peace will reign again in Gebal. As for his posterity they will be cut off by the sword.'

It is the Egyptian mind which speaks, afraid that the body is the life-line to the soul. At Byblos the cults of Osiris and Adonis mingled, and Plutarch says that Osiris was placed as a wooden column in the Byblian king's palace, where the bases for wooden pillars remain; and Isis, searching for him, wept at the well which served the city for three thousand years, and which still keeps its spiral steps and a sad beauty.

So the myth went down familiar paths and won acceptance, and Lucian said that 'some of the inhabitants of Byblus maintain that the Egyptian Osiris is buried in their town, and that the public mourning and secret rites are performed in memory not of Adonis, but of Osiris'.

But this was not so, for all the land of Byblos is filled with remembrance of Adonis. Walking the mountains behind the town, I found villages grown from shrines on the high places, so many that the whole hinterland must have been populous. Especially in the mellow, patinated churches does the ancient stone appear, and Greek inscriptions are in the walls unread, and Maronite priests with catholic reverence lay broken statuary upon their altars.

Inscribed Greek stones are used as lintels, esteemed for the angular beauty of their letters, or thought to be Christian; so

* 'Gebal' was the Semitic name for Byblos; it is still called 'Jebail', 'Small Mountain'.

that I entered the church of St Elias at Belaat under the blasphemy:
'Aspasios, son of Dionysius, dedicated this to Greatest Zeus.'

St Elias, or Elijah, who killed the priests of Baal, has shrines
along the littoral, for he was sovereign against the return of the
elder gods; and St George, usurping Adonis, is everywhere. So
these churches are set among the hills by the genius of a pagan
world, where the landscape serves them best, united and com-
pleting one another. It is the exception for a village not to own
Roman stones, some statue, wine-press or tomb. Even the
church altars are sometimes older than Christ, and the inscription of St George's, near Amschit, reads now with a faint,
crestfallen note of resentment: 'I, Secundus, son of Boethion,
dedicated the altar to Zeus.'

Near Ghineh in the mountains south of Byblos is a Roman
temple which the people call 'the Palace of Adonis'. The god is
carved upon a sheaf of rock, where tombs are sunk and filled with
water, looking looking across a tree-spread valley. His legend
stretches in three worn panels above the grave. On one side a
person stands in an attitude of calm with a lance in his hand;
he is dressed in a girdled tunic for the chase, and beside him,
confirmed by their long bodies and the rise and dip of their
tails, are hounds in profile.

So Adonis departs for the hunt, and in the centre tableau leans
his spear against the attack of a wild beast. To the right a woman
is seated on a throne, and although her head is obliterated and the
stone decayed, she seems to be bowed in mourning, with her
left arm raised to her face. 'On Mount Lebanon', wrote
Macrobius at the end of the fourth century A.D., 'Venus is
represented with veiled head, sad air, supporting with her left
hand her face hidden in her mantle, and apparently in tears. This
statue . . . represents the earth during winter, when it is numb
and sunless.'*

Deeper in the valley these motifs are repeated with the care
given to cult figures, and doubtless there were many more,
carved as prayers for resurrection where this upland glade,
crinkled and peaceful as a cupped hand, slips into the mountains
of Adonis.

'The Mourning Aphrodite' was found again near Tripolis,

* Some scholars have not seen Adonis in the Ghineh sculptures, and suggest
them as a simple funeral monument. The beast which attacks the hunter, they
say, has the stance and maneless head of a bear, not a boar. But the coinci-
dences seem too many, and the animal is a composite creature with a ghostly
tusk, reared in a stance which neatly fills the artist's panel.

exactly as Macrobius describes her, carved free-standing out of limestone, less than four inches high and oddly proportioned: a late Seleucid work with a melancholy charm. She shows by her ornamental size that the goddess was a token for every day, a household talisman. This statue, perhaps, was ancestor to the Christian *Mater Dolorosa*; and a Pompeian fresco in which she supports across her knees the dead Adonis, limp and gashed in the side, may have been the prototype for the Christian *Pietà*.

*   *   *

The great humanist Ernest Renan was the first to excavate the Byblos country. In the house of Zakhia Tobea at Amschit he spent the early 1860's, probing the 'holy and enchanted' hills and making excavations, with his sister Henriette, his quiet genius.

'The whole spirit of the ancient Syrian worship seemed to rise up before us. Byblos lay at our feet; southward, in the sacred region of the Lebanon, rose the strangely jagged outline of the rocks and forest of Djebel-Mousa, which legend denotes as the spot where Adonis perished. . . .'

The old house is the same, a mansion of cool darkness, its marble halls recessed in the classic Syrian style, while across the windows the jacaranda and hibiscus shine. The Tobea family, who are courteous as in Renan's day, show his letters and photographs. Henriette died of fever here, and was buried in a walled sepulchre, open to the sky.

'The villagers, who had grown much attached to her, followed her bier. There was no possibility of embalming the corpse; some temporary resting-place had to be found, at the end of the village, near a pretty chapel. . . . I shrink from the idea of taking her from the beautiful mountains. . . .'

There he left her. Inside the tomb grows a giant oak tree, which must have pleased his pagan soul, and the Maronite chapel remains to satisfy her Christian one, where priestly chanting turns the dusk to night.

'We know not the exact relationship between great souls and the principle of Eternity. . . .'

*   *   *

The fishing villages are unspoilt along the Byblos coast, and there is an Ottoman doziness and permanence about their green-watered coves, idle with fishing-boats. Fidar is one of these, and its peninsula, almost an island, is a natural stroke of theatre, with a handsome church upon it and a rough, old chapel. On its seaward side the waves fall among pools, and rocks which have been torn from the shore are half-submerged. Few people come, because of the sea, but candles have been left in one of the grottoes, and nursing mothers take the water which drips from its moss-covered ceiling and touch it to their breasts.

So evident a shrine for the renewal of life must belong to the goddess, and the Phoenicians cannot have neglected the harbour behind, which would have been deeper than now. There is a suggestion of carving about the boulders, though this may be the sculpture of the sea, and along the coast are wave-smoothed cisterns, vaults and quarries, Adonis-haunted, where children are brought for healing.

From Byblos at this time, when the Roman fleets sailed and the civil wars were over, temples and porticoes fanned outward to the hills, and a few poor columns still run like light above the necropolis.

Near the citadel a small theatre was uncovered, standing on older ruins, and was transplanted to a ledge above the sea. From the Semitic sorcery of tombs, with their fetishes and imprecations, one comes upon it suddenly with enchantment: a horseshoe of dazzling stone, turned on itself with a happy esteem of man. One walks in quiet across its cobbled orchestra, and is grateful for it. In the first tier of seats are holes where wooden lances upheld an awning. Tiny, pedimented niches are set against the stage wall on the ground, complete but for their gods. The proscenium is the sea.

In this modest compass the Roman kept his world, no doubt building for Syrian merchants, but in his own pattern and with his careful thought. The head of Bacchus, spread in mosaic across the orchestra, is almost Botticellian in beauty; not the coarse god of a later tradition, but a wreathed angel. He is successor to the Greek Dionysus, who symbolized the fruits of the earth and the ripening sun, and like Adonis he died and returned. 'It is said that the beautiful Adonis is none other than Dionysus.' So Plutarch writes, adding a new fibre to the strange web, and it is true that in some parts of the Mediterranean Adonis was seen as the infernal form of Dionysus: 'I am Bacchus among the living, Adonis among the dead.'

However this may be, the Adonis cults declined in other lands as Christianity took hold. The Greeks, who transformed Astarte, had always been suspicious of the consort who kept her pure, and they added nothing to his worship but the grace of legend and an elegiac praise.

'Woe! woe for Cypris!' moans the mountain steep;
Oaks in the forest moan Adonis' ills;
For Aphrodite all the rivers weep;
And all the little springs in all the hills.

Even in Bion's idylls the Adonia of the Greeks are permeated by a decorous languor, and the statues portray pretty youths holding perfume and myrrh. Already by the third century A.D. the festival of Adonis, if Theocritus writes truly, is decadent in Alexandria. Figures of the god and goddess are laid out in the palace of the Ptolemies. They embrace on a purple-covered couch in ritual marriage, overhung with arbours and cupids, and the next day are committed to the sea and mourned as dead. The festival is a social occasion, and the two Syracusan women whom Theocritus portrays are not concerned with its meaning:

'What a crowd—packed tight,
And pushing like pigs!'
'Praxinoe, hush! She's about to sing the "Adonis Psalm"—
The prima donna—came out from Argos: she took the palm
For the "Dirge" last year; so she, I'm perfectly certain, will sing
Something fine. . . .'

The cult at Alexandria outlasted the fourth century, long after the empire was Christian, until the pagan life-blood flowed in other veins, and the last temples were closed. As late as the tenth century, Christian Syrians, in a festival called Ta'uz, threw the ashes of a 'god' into the wind, sacrificed pigs and honoured St George as a being killed and resurrected many times. But in the west Adonis passed peacefully from the idylls of Theocritus to Shakespeare and Milton; and Astarte, generally discreet as the classical Venus, became an emblem of beauty for half the world.

Gently she withdrew her identity, confiding in remote places, and other towns robbed Byblos of history, until the Crusaders came and built their castle and the Church of St John, a jewel in autumnal stone. They built with a delicate austerity, and gave Byblos something light and strong in the pillared spareness of its aisles, its colonetted windows and domed baptistery, cut with the grave ornament of the Genoese romanesque. Sixty years ago an ornate belfry was added where the texture of the stone had been ornament enough, but that is all.

The last Crusader sea-tower dabbles in the waves, placed to throw chains across the harbour mouth where the town wall ended. The whole port has an ageing richness, flowing out from Roman stone, all harmony and quiet; the fishing-boats sighing on the sun in the water, the forever drying nets. Against the Crusader rampart the waves make weak commotion, then vanish on the harbour water with a faint surprised ripple.

Looking down from the tower, stray columns appear beneath the surface, and gold Phoenician coins are there for those who dive to them. One sees the littleness of the harbour, its entrance only twenty yards across, where the beaked ships went out with papyrus and the first olive tree to Greece; and the Greeks called their books 'byblia' after the city which sent them paper, and passed the name to the Bible.

Perhaps nowhere on earth are so many generations fused, and if Byblos tells anything, it is that death itself is the token of renewal. 'When a man hath done, then he beginneth. . . .' As the goddess held in her hands the seed and the decay, and as her rites were intermingled joy and sorrow, so the ruins of Byblos bring this eastern view to mind, in a profile of peace.

The Arab has a sense of being part of a whole, and is able to accept it; and because of impermanence, because rest is illusion, and life an endless becoming, he takes and enjoys the fullness of a moment in the stride of his nature, if not as his philosophy. 'Men', says the Sufi, 'are but waves on the sea of God.'

Byblos is an intimation of the search's end. It places the cool order of colonnade and theatre against the dark, magic graves, as if the dignity of reason could live in peace with the bigotry of faith. By this contrast, among the ruins and in the mind, it condemns them by one another—reason as fragile and faith as blind—so that only by man realizing his powerlessness can he continue pilgrimage, without knowing how he may recognize his holy city.

I slid into the sea at night and swam. Near the harbour the empty boats breathed, and the Crusader world was heavy and soft behind: the church and the blunt castle, religion and war. The moon was shining. The waves flowed in my fingers like liquid gold, and drunken fish went spangled under rocks. To the north I saw the darkness where the river of Adonis meets the sea.

15. The Scarlet River

He is made one with Nature: there is heard
His voice in all her music, from the moan
Of thunder, to the song of night's sweet bird;
He is a presence to be felt and known
In darkness and in light, from herb and stone,
Spreading itself where'er that Power may move
Which has withdrawn his being to its own . . .
P. B. Shelley: *Adonais*

THE WAY TO APHACA begins where the mountains widen and release the Adonis river in the sea. Near its mouth are caves whose entrances were cut and smoothed for gates, closed with fig trees now, but betrayed as sacred by their carefully carved niches and complex chambers.

This was the first station on the pilgrim's way, where worshippers turned inland along the crags above the river, until the road lost sight of the sea and the valley closed round them. Their goal was the source of the Adonis waters, where a temple stood which was old in Lucian's day, called by the Greeks 'Aphaca', 'the Kiss'. Here Adonis and Astarte first loved in legend, and the god hunted and died where the great river flows from the mountain.

'There is yet another wonderful thing at Byblos', says Lucian. 'A river has its source in the mountain of Lebanon and flows into the sea. It bears the name Adonis. Every year it loses its colour and takes on the colour of blood. At its mouth it dyes the sea red over a large area. Thus are the people of Byblos informed that it is time to go into mourning. They say at that time that Adonis is wounded.' And Henry Maundrell, at the end of the seventeenth century, wrote that: 'Upon the bank of this Stream. . . . we had a very tempestuous night both of Wind, and Rain, almost without cessation, and with so great violence, that our Servants were hardly able to keep our Tents over us . . . by this means we had the fortune to see that this Stream, at certain seasons of the Year, especially about the feast of Adonis, is of a bloody colour. . . . Something like this we actually saw come to pass.'

Even in Lucian's time a sceptic attributed the change to the red earth at the river's mouth, and geologists say that when the spring rains come, they carry the soil down to the river and discolour it. But science cannot be trusted to recognize the blood of a god, and the Phoenicians, who understood, must have cupped this magic in their hands and known that the earth and blood were one.

They made their pilgrimage while the last winter rains were scarlet in the sea, and perhaps in June also, when the Adonia were celebrated in other parts of the east. The earth dies then, its depth and bloom of colour washed away, and the mountains hold a naked radiance. The sea unfurled behind me like a part of the sky. Among flowerless rocks the crickets grated like the dulled cry of the earth, and blades of corn clashed across the slopes. The god was dying in a long passion, with gasps of morning wind and all life fading; yet I could understand how Renan called this country the loveliest in the world, and why the Egyptians thought it the land of the gods.

Spring pilgrims, wending above the river, found the whole valley green, and from the cliffs the streams spun down through air, too far for sound, and overspreading hills the anemones showed crimson, while many hundred feet below, the river moaned and splashed its sacrament against the rocks.

Machnaqa is half-way to Aphaca, and pilgrims, at the end of their first day's march, must have spent the cold night there. The hills conceal the temple to the last. Then suddenly it is there, filled with light and flowers, as if awaiting resurrection. A plain pilastered wall has half-fallen round it, and in the enclosure grows a green mist of corn where goats move unseen, and broken columns stand.

The shrine is only a fragment—four columns holding entablatures against the sanctuary wall, crowned with a balustrade, rough in execution. But ruin has lent it a chance perfection; what was once heavy and corrupt now slenderness and grace: a temple for a shepherd or a king. By it the rocks descend to the abyss, and the river banks, too steep for goats, are soft in oak and juniper. The earth surges and drops weightlessly, rolling into gorges and heaped against itself in far descending spurs, crowding the river.

To the north a corridor leads through rock to a necropolis; and sculptured on each side, but very worn, Adonis appears again with the mourning Aphrodite, keeping their hope in the pathway to the dead. They are carved in Ionic frames and he, facing west with one arm extended, walks among blurred lesser persons. Aphrodite is seated, with her elbows thrust forward on her lap and her left hand raised to her face, weeping. Her hair appears bunched high, and she may have been crowned; and although her pose is elementary and half-effaced, the impression of grief is indelible in the bowed head and upraised arm.

These carvings are the work of a poor people buried in the savage tombs beyond. Machnaqa reflects the dying classical world in its crude craftsmanship and the loose construction of the temple, which was perhaps never finished. All that is known of the holy valley comes from late Roman times, and as I sat in the half-shade of the pass, it was the classical, the personal, view of the legend which touched me: the man who died, and the woman who loved.

Meliton, who first wrote of Aphaca, associated Astarte with Balthi, Queen of Cyprus, and Tammuz with a Phoenician king who was killed by her husband; 'and from that time Balthi remained in Gebal, and she died in the city Aphaca, where Tammuz was buried'. So the myth descends from cosmic forces to ordinary men, and makes this also the country of love. The myth can never be accepted simply; and even the fusing of the divine and the mortal is natural where Asia, the continent of gods, meets the Mediterranean, the sea of men.

Higher up are the ruins of a Byzantine church built from the stones of a temple to Adonis, stained grey and brown as the wind has found or overlooked them. It is dedicated, of course, to St George, whom shepherds call *Mar Jurios Azraq*, 'St George the Blue', but they have taken most of it away and left a pilastered shell with Roman doorways.

Bandits and killers take refuge in these mountains, and behind Akura village the secret passage, once used by Astarte's pilgrims, leads to the lake of Yammouneh. Now the valley-bowl lifts far above the track, rough and undulant, and pencilled with trees on its higher slopes. The cliffs are grand and calm, and be-yond, even in June, the snow shines on the mountains.

The way ends. Tributary streams pour from all sides as if the valley were a burst cistern, and leave their sudden greenness on the rocks, where the last anemones grow and the temple of Aphaca lies in ruin.

One stands here reverent to more than beauty; the rock mass sheer above seven hundred feet, carved with temple faces by the air. From its base, out of the cave's secret, the green river comes, descending by cascades into wide, angry pools, rounded and made calmer by the arts of early men. Here they offered gifts to the goddess, who would receive them into her waters in token of acceptance, or leave them floating on the surface if rejected, 'and not only cloth and such substances, but even gold, silver or other of those materials which usually sink'.* And on the first night of festival, the goddess and the god were mystically united, for 'a fire like a star descended from the top of Lebanon and sunk into the neighbouring river; they affirm that this was Urania, for they call Aphrodite by this name.'†

'This was a grove and temple', wrote Eusebius, 'not situated in the midst of any city . . . but apart from the beaten and frequented road, at Aphaca, on part of the summit of Mount Libanus, and dedicated to the foul demon known by the name of Venus.' The emperor Constantine, 'judging that such a temple was unfit for the light of heaven, gave orders that the building with its offerings should be utterly destroyed'. But only at the end of the fourth century, in the reign of Arcadius, was the cult of Aphaca silenced. St John Chrysostom inspired an armed invasion of the valley, and the pagans took up swords and fought for their shrines and were slain, or carried their religion underground.

This violence is remembered in the humped wreck of the sanctuary and in the stones which slide beneath it to the river; but the blocks are dappled with the beauty of old people, and trees have leapt from their crevices. As I walked along the edge of its destruction, I saw a sunken tower with a ruined pyramidal roof, like the one at Qalat Fakra; but its mystery is well-kept, the stones in tumult, and plants underfoot send up raw, hurt scents.

The sanctuary had been built with toil, for in the rubble is a rose-granite column—the last of several brought from Egypt. The walls lie as they were felled, jointed in waves of stone untouched, as if their overthrow had been delicate and the temple left unplundered for a millennium and a half. Probably the soldiers of Chrysostom undermined the walls as they drove away the last worshippers, so that the cult vanished before the next century was past; and here it seemed the goddess died, where Adonis was buried, and passed into oblivion.

But the temple is Aphaca itself, not the stones which were laid there. It would have been sacred in any time, for any people. A part of the river still runs under the ruined tower, where it

* Zosimus: *Historia.*
† Hermias Sozomen: *Historia Ecclesiastica.*

'The Cedars of the Lord'

Machnaqa

Aphaca: the source

was channelled darkly, and above it, breaking from the walls, is a wide-armed fig tree. Pieces from the robes of sick people are tied to the branches as charms for healing. Beside it a passage, large enough only for a child to enter, is cluttered with votive candles and a faded figure of the Virgin holding an anemone. Often at dusk a villager will come to pray, with a candle in a bottle, and stepping carefully onto the ledge above the river, places his gift in the recess.

They say these lights are given to 'Sitt el Matrah', the Lady of the Place. The Christians think of her as the Virgin; the Moslems call her, mysteriously, *Zahra*, and they worship her equally, though she comes to them unknown from fifteen centuries. She haunts the pools where the sick are brought at summer, and visits men in dreams, and heals, and grants fertility to women. But she no longer demands a sacrifice; she is gentle and ghostly, and as ever enigmatic, giving half answers or keeping silent.

The quest is over; the valley rock holds up its hand. From it the everlasting waters spring, where in the pastoral legend the goddess cradled in her arms the dying god, who never dies. The Phoenicians sheared the cave ceiling smooth and built a vanished temple in its mouth above the Aphaca waters. The river flows from galleries of darkness, turned one upon the other, and the pilgrim can follow the goddess no further. She withdraws behind the senselessness of the dark, reflecting only the minds which search for her. The quest for God discloses men. But the ancients saw this as a sign: life out of stone. 'Unto the place from whence the rivers come, thither they return again.' Nothing ends, but sinks with grief and patience underground, awaiting its time.

Yet even the worm or leaf is resurrected as a different form. New life may take old patterns, but never again does it reproduce the mind, the look, the cadence of a voice, as it had once been. And we, who love the individual, recoil from this, and hope the men of Byblos kept their spirit when they went with weapons from their graves.

But the eastern concept is larger, gives man a part in God, picking him up when he has died, like the fragment of a broken dish, and placing him back in the Whole. The goddess teaches him ignorance, for his own hands and breath are a mystery to him and the only divinities he overthrows are those which he has created.

The dream of finding does not fade. Because time is corruptible, the past may come again, and the figures of love return. But pilgrims, all passing the same way, direct their gaze ahead and put their trust in the miracles they know. And although they leave the cavern by the way they entered, they see Adonis rising with the spring breeze of flutes and cymbals, and feel the frailness of their feet on the shell of the earth.

SELECT BIBLIOGRAPHY

Atallah, Wahib. *Adonis dans la littérature et l'Art Grec.* (Librairie C. Klincksieck, Paris, 1966)

Attwater, Donald. *The Christian Churches of the East.* (Thomas More Books, 1961)

Baramki, Dimitri. *Phoenicia and the Phoenicians.* (Khayats, Beirut, 1961)

Bliss, Frederick Jones. *The Religions of Modern Syria and Palestine.* (Charles Scribner's Sons, New York, 1912)

Boulanger, Robert. *The Lebanon.* (Hachette, 1965)

Bouron, N. *Les Druzes.* (Éditions Berger-Levrault, Paris, 1930)

Burckhardt, John Lewis. *Travels in Syria and the Holy Land.* (John Murray, 1822)

Burton, Richard F. and Drake, C. F. T. *Unexplored Syria.* 2 vols. (Tinsley Bros., London, 1872)

Chasseaud, G. W. *The Druses of the Lebanon.* (Richard Bentley, London, 1855)

Churchill, C. H. *The Druzes and the Maronites under the Turkish Rule from 1840 to 1860.* (Bernard Quarite, London, 1862)

— *Mount Lebanon.* 3 vols. (Saunders and Otley, London, 1853)

Condé, Bruce. *See Lebanon.* (Harb Bijjani Press, Beirut, 1960)

Contenau, G. *La Civilisation Phénicienne.* (Payot, Paris, 1926)

Deschamps, Paul. *Les Châteaux des Croisés en Terre-Sainte.* (Librairie Orientaliste Paul Geuthner, Paris, 1939)

Dunand, Maurice. *Fouilles de Byblos.* 2 vols. (Librairie Orientaliste Paul Geuthner, Paris, 1939)

Dussaud, René. *Topographie historique de la Syrie Antique et Médiévale.* (Librairie Orientaliste Paul Geuthner, Paris, 1927)

Farnell, Lewis. *Cults of the Greek States.* 3 vols. (Oxford, Clarendon Press, 1896)

Fedden, Robin. *Syria and Lebanon.* (Robert Hale, 1955)

Fedden, Robin, and Thomson, John. *Crusader Castles.* (John Murray, 1950)

Frazer, Sir James George. *The Golden Bough. Part IV. Adonis, Attis, Osiris.* (University Books, New York, 1961)

Fyfe, Theodore. *Hellenistic Architecture.* (Cambridge University Press, 1937)

Gulick, John. 'Conservatism and Change in a Lebanese Village.' *The Middle East Journal*, Vol. 8, No. 3, 1954

— 'The Lebanese Village: an Introduction.' *The American Anthropologist*, Vol. 55, No. 3

Haslip, Joan. *Lady Hester Stanhope.* (Cobden-Sanderson, London, 1934)

Hitti, Philip K. *Lebanon in History.* (Macmillan & Co. Ltd., London, 1962)

— *The Origins of the Druze People and Religion.* (Columbia University Press, 1928)

Hourani, A. H. *Minorities in the Arab World.* (Oxford University Press, 1947)

Huxley, Julian. *From an Antique Land.* (Max Parrish & Co., 1954)

Izzard, Ralph and Molly. *Smelling the Breezes: A Journey through the High Lebanon.* (Hodder & Stoughton, 1959)

James, E. O. *Christian Myth and Ritual.* (John Murray, 1933)

— *The Cult of the Mother Goddess.* (Thames & Hudson, 1959)

Jamil, Ruhi. *Beirut and the Republic of Lebanon.* (Librairie Universelle, Beirut, 1948)

Jones, A. H. M. *Cities of the Eastern Roman Provinces.* (Clarendon Press, 1937)

— *The Herods of Judaea.* (Oxford University Press, 1938)

Khayat, Mary, and Keatinge, Margaret. *Lebanon, Land of the Cedars.* (Khayats, Beirut, 1960)

Lamartine, Alphonse de. *Travels in the East.* (W. & R. Chambers, London, 1839)

Lucian. *The Syrian Goddess.* Trs. Prof. Herbert A. Strong. (Constable & Co., London, 1913)

Parfit, J. T. *Druzes and the Secret Sects of Syria.* (Lay Reader Headquarters, Westminster, 1917)

Poidebard, A. *Un Grand Port Disparu: Tyr.* (Librairie Orientaliste Paul Geuthner, Paris, 1939)

Poidebard, A. and Lauffray, J. *Sidon: Aménagements antiques du Port de Saida.* (Ministère des Travaux Publics, Beirut, 1951)

Porter, J. L. *Handbook for Syria and Palestine.* (1875)

Renan, Ernest. *Mission en Phénicie.* (Imprimerie Impériale, 1864)

Robinson, Edward. *Biblical Researches in Palestine.* (John Murray, 1867)

Seltzer, Carl C. *Contributions to the Racial Anthropology of the Near East.* (Peabody Museum, Harvard University, 1940)

Tannous, Afif I. 'Group Behaviour in the Village Community of Lebanon.' *The American Journal of Sociology*, Vol. XLVIII, No. 2

— 'The Village in the National Life of Lebanon.' *The Middle East Journal*, Vol. 3, No. 2, April 1949

Thomson, W. M. *The Land and the Book.* (Thomas Nelson & Sons, 1910)

Urquhart, David. *The Lebanon.* (Thomas Cautley Newby, 1860)

Vellay, Charles. *Le Culte et les Fêtes d'Adonis-Thammouz dans l'Orient Antique.* (Ernest Leroux, Paris, 1904)

Warmington, E. H. *Greek Geography*. (J. M. Dent & Sons, Ltd.)

Wiegand, Theodor. *Baalbek*. (Berlin and Leipzig, 1921)

William, Archbishop of Tyre. *A History of Deeds done beyond the Sea*. (Columbia University Press, 1943)

Index

Caucasus, 153
Ceres, Festival of, 151
Chalcedon, Council of, 58
Chalcis, 90, 110, 111, 112
Chalcolithic man, 115, 149
Chaldean, 103
Chalus, 130
Chams, Sitt es-, 75
Chamoun, Asaad, 73, 74, 75
    President Camille, 73, 74
    family, 73
Charife, Abbas, 128, 129, 130, 131
Charifi family, 129, 130
Charities, The, 22
Charlemagne, Emperor, 91
Chateaubrand, 42
Chebab dynasty, 71, 72, 75
Cheops, 151
Children of Israel, 103
Chlifa, 127, 129
Christ, Jesus, 18, 26, 55, 68, 89, 91,
    95, 133, 140, 143, 151
Christ-Roi Monastery, 101, 102
'Christian' (Bunyan), 96
Christians, 7–8, 17, 38, 51, 57, 68,
    72, 75, 91, 92, 114, 121, 129, 131,
    132, 134, 135, 136–7, 138, 145,
    158, 165
Cilicia, 28
Cinyrus, King of Byblos, 151
Cinyrus, King of Cyprus, 26
Claudius, Emperor, 94, 111
Cleopatra, Queen, 110
Cnidus, 22, 23
Coele Syria, 2, 110
Comnenos, Emperor Manuel, 145
Conrad of Montferrat, 28, 38
Constantine, Emperor, 121, 164
Constantinople, 18, 37, 52, 76; also
    see Istanbul
Convent of Mars Elias, 63
Corinth, 22
Cornwall, 5
Corunna, 63
Crassus, 77
Cratinus, 26
Crusaders, 4, 10, 11, 19, 28, 33, 37,
    38, 44, 45, 48, 52, 55, 56, 66, 76,
    79, 102, 141, 144, 145, 146, 147,
    149, 158
Cuthites, 79
Cybele, 73, 117
Cypris, 158
Cyprus, 21, 22, 26, 47, 48, 55, 90,
    101, 104, 116, 136, 146, 151
Cyrus, King, 79

Cytherea, 22

Damascus, Damascenes, 3, 32, 39,
    40, 43, 44, 45, 53, 58, 62, 72,
    75, 84, 102, 103, 110, 111, 138,
    145, 146
    Pasha of, 45
Damour, 87
David, King, 134
Deir el Kamar, 70, 71, 72, 73, 74
Deir es Salib, 141
Deir es Sitt, see Monastery of Joun
Deir Machmouche, see Machmouche
    Monastery
Deir Moukalles, see Monastery of
    the Holy Saviour
Delphi, 22
Derusaiaioi, 79
Dido, Queen, 6
Diman, 140
Diomedes, 22
Dione, 22
Dionysus, 117, 157
Diwani (script), 40
Djebel-Mousa, 156
Djezzar Pasha, 28
Dog River (Lycus), 31, 90, 92, 96,
    101, 102, 103, 105
    Valley, 92, 96
Dostoyevsky, Feodor, 41
Douahi family, 141
    Patriarch, 143
Dreux, Comte de, 79
Druse Hills, 31
Druses, 51, 52, 55, 57, 67, 68, 69,
    72, 73, 78, 79, 81, 83, 84, 85, 86
Dryden, John, 77, 78
Dushara, 114

Edessa, 79
Egypt, -ians, 4, 5, 10, 14, 35, 40, 57,
    87, 96, 102, 103, 104, 112, 116,
    131, 133, 134, 137, 150, 152, 153,
    162, 164
Egyptian Harbour (Sidon), 10
Ehden, 144
Ejbeh, 144
El., see under next name
Eleanor de Montfort, 38
Elias, Church of St., 155; see also
    Elijah
Elijah, 19, 155
England, English, 27, 33, 40, 42, 63,
    78, 82, 92
Eros, 22
Esarhaddon, King, 79, 104

Lycus, *see* Dog river

Maanid Dynasty, 70, 71
Maaser-es-Chouf, 83, 84, 85, 86
Machmouche Monastery, 53–62
Machnaqa, 162, 163
Macrobius, 119, 155, 156
Magianism, 68
Mahmoud of Sidon, 8, 9, 10, 11, 12
Mahomet, 42
Mahomet Ali, 63, 75, 76
Mamelukes, 11, 44, 146
Mantara, 17, 18
Mar Abda Monastery, 101
Mar Antun Bedawi, 142
Mar Bahonna, 141
Mar Jurios Azraq, 163
Mar Sarkis, 141
Marduk (Babylonian god), 103, 134
Marina, St, 142, 143
Mark, St, 28
Maron, St, Monastery of, 55
Maronites, 51, 54, 55, 67, 70, 72, 89,
    92, 101, 133, 140, 142, 143, 154
Mars (Roman god), 91
Mars Elias, Convent of, 63
Mary, The Virgin, 17, 60, 73, 74,
    85, 109, 140, 143, 165
Mater Dolorosa, 156
Maundrell, Henry, 52, 134, 161
Mauretania, 5
Mecca, 40, 42
Media and Medes, 79, 107
Medinah, 42
Mejdel Anjar, 111
Melhem, Emir, 72
Melisende of Toulouse, 145, 146
Meliton, 163
Melkites, 58, 60
Melqart, 4, 21
Memnon, Colossus of, 102
Menelaus, 5
Mercury (Roman god), 118, 119
    -Adonis, 122
Mesopotamia, 5
Messiah, The, 63
Messiah (of Dog River), 96, 97
Metawilleh (Shia), 28, 31, 32, 33,
    36, 40, 57
Metulleh, 43
Meyrouba, 97
Mezraa, El, 34
Michaud, Général, 69
Michaelangelo, 11
Miletus, 61
Milk, River of, 95, 96

Milly, Stephanie de, 37
Milton, John, 77, 158
Miyumiye, 9
Moab, 114
Moloch, *see* Melqart
Monastery of Antoura, 101
    Christ-Roi, 101, 102
    the Gazelle, 115
    the Holy Saviour, 58, 59, 62, 63,
        65, 67
    Joun, 62–5
    Louaiza, 101
    Machmouche, 53–62
    Mar Abda, 101
    Our Lady, 57, 58, 66, 73
    Qubbet el Bedawi, 147
    Saint Maron, 55
    Sarba, 106, 107
Mongols, 84
Montreal Castle, 38
Moore, Sir John, 63
Moors, 74
Moses, 79
Moslems, 28, 31, 33, 36, 52, 56, 57,
    68, 72, 104, 114, 120, 122, 129,
    135, 136, 137, 138, 142, 144, 146,
    147, 148, 165
Mouchtara, 79, 82
Mount of Pilgrims, 144
Muadhem, Sultan, 38
Murex (snail), 11, 24
Mutatio ad Nonum, 19
Myrrha, 26, 151

Nabateans, 114
Nahr el Leban, 95, 96
Nahr el Litani, *see* Litani river
Naphtali, 90
Napoleon Bonaparte, 76
Napoleon III, 103
Naski (script), 40
Nasser, President, 41, 82, 137, 138
Nasr, Athanasi, 58
Navarino, Battle of, 63
Nebi Ayyoub, 56
    Azar, 56
    Hanania, 56
    Misha (tomb of), 56
    Shiit, 115
    Younes, 10
Nebuchadnezzar II, 21, 102
Niha, 47, 115, 116
Niha, Jebel, 47
Niha-Toron, 51, 52, 66
Nile, river, 74
Nimrod (tomb of), 115

Sannin, Mount, 31, 88, 89, 90, 92, 95, 96, 114, 115
Sappho, 22, 152
Saracens, 11, 37, 38
Sarafand, *see* Sarepta
Sarba, Monastery at, 106, 107
Sarepta, 2, 19
Sargon of Assyria, 21, 107
Sartre, Jean Paul, 41
Saudi Arabia, 9
Sayette, 10, 43, 45
Scorpio, 91
Scythia, 74
Sea, Mediterranean, 54, 104, 136, 163
Sea, Red, 53
Secundus, son of Boethion 155,
Seleucids, 110, 117
Seljuk Turks, *see* Turks
Semites, 1, 6, 91
Sennacherib, 21, 106
Serapis, 107
Seth (tomb of), 115
Sepulchre, the Holy, 98
Severus, Emperor Septimius, 117
Shakespeare, William, 77, 78, 158
'Shalaboun', 41
Shelley, Percy Bysshe, 161
Shia, 68
Shiites, 33
Sidon, -ians, 2, 3, 4, 6, 7, 8, 9, 10, 11, 13, 14, 17, 18, 27, 34, 43, 45, 52, 53, 60, 63, 66, 71, 72, 81, 87, 110, 137, 144
Sidonian Harbour, Tyre, 10, 11, 20
Simkaniye, 77, 82
Sinai, 112, 116
Sisters of St Joseph, 3–4
'Sitt el Matrah', 165
Socrates Scholasticus, 121
Solomon, King, 32, 56, 83, 117
Solomon, Temple of, 20, 83, 134
Sozomen, Hermias, 164n
Spain, 5
Sparta, 22
'Spring of 40 Martyrs', 130
Stanhope, Lady Hester, 62–4, 65, 75, 82, 122
Stendhal, 99
Stephanie d'Oultrejordain, 38
Stourhead Gardens, 122
Strabo (geographer), 10, 19, 21, 110, 144
Sudan, 150
Sufi, 159
'Sun of Righteousness, The', 91

Swedes, 135
Syracuse, 27, 158
Syria, -ians, 3, 10, 17, 40, 47, 63, 66, 66, 67, 69, 73, 86, 93, 102, 111, 112, 117, 131, 132, 133, 135, 138, 145, 147, 157
Syria, Hollow, *see* Coele Syria
Syriac language, 55, 89, 140, 141
Syrian Desert, 6, 113
   Goddess, 120n, 151, 152n
   Hills, 44

Tabnit, King, 14
Tacitus, 8
Tamerlane, 84
Tammuz, 6, 7, 25, 153, 163; *see also* Adonis
Tanuk Dynasty, 70
Tarshish, 5, 90
Taurus Mountains, 3
Ta'uz Festival, 158
Tel Aviv, 39
Tel el Buraq, 19
Telemachus, 5
Tel Maashuq, 25
Thales of Miletus, 61, 66
Theocritus, 17, 158
Theodora, Princess, 37
Theodosius, Emperor, 121, 143
Thessaly, 48
Thoas, 5
'Through the Looking Glass', 59
Tiberias, 37, 146
Tiberius, Emperor, 11
Tibnin (Toron), 37
Tiglath-Pileser, 107
Titus, Emperor, 111
Tobea, Zakhia, 156
Tobruk, 8
Tolstoy, Leonid, 41
Totou, Father Abrahim, 58
Toron, Castle of, 38, 40, 44
Tortosa, 11
Toulouse, *see* Bertrand Raymond
Trablus, *see* Tripolis
Trachonitis, 110
Trajan, Emperor, 53, 119
Tripoli, *see* Tripolis
Tripolis, 3, 71, 135, 137, 139, 144, 145, 146, 147, 155
   Counts of, *see* Bertrand Raymond
   Princess of, 79
Troezen, 22
Turkey, Turks, 6, 36, 37, 45, 71, 72, 102, 134, 140
Turks, Ottoman, 8, 51, 52, 63